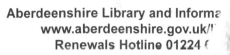

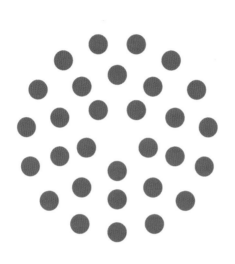

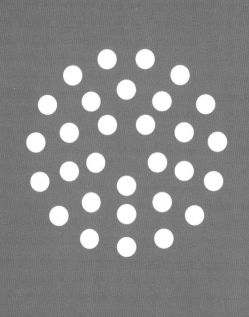

spice it

MURDOCH BOOKS

contents

the spice of life

Imagine a world without spices — no gingerbread or gin, vanilla ice cream or licorice; curries would be bland, spicy dishes would lack the bite of chilli and mulled wine would be a simple glass of warm red. Spices are used around the world, and in every cuisine, to enhance or highlight the flavours in a dish — from snacks and nibbles to mains, desserts and baked treats.

Today the abundance and availability of spices, and their relatively low cost, are in stark contrast to their scarcity and immense cost in the past. For thousands of years, spices were luxury items that only the very wealthy could afford. The spice trade, which developed from ever-increasing demands, eventually grew into a worldwide industry. As testament to the importance and value of spices, the East India Company (1600–1873) became not only the largest spice trader in the world but also a potent political force.

what are spices?

Spices are the aromatic berries (peppercorns), fruits (paprika), buds (cloves), roots (ginger), seeds (caraway), or bark (cinnamon) of a variety of plants, most of which are indigenous to tropical countries. Saffron, the hand-picked stigmas from a tropical plant, is also considered a spice — and is the world's most expensive. Herbs, by contrast, are generally the leaves, flowers, and sometimes the stems, of aromatic, non-woody plants. Some single plant varieties, such as coriander (cilantro), can provide both a herb and a spice. The leaves, stems and roots of coriander (cilantro) are considered a herb, while the seeds of the plant are a popular spice.

harvesting spices

The method of growing and harvesting spices depends upon the particular spice. Obtaining some spices, such as vanilla beans and saffron threads, involves a complex, time-consuming and labour-intensive process. Other spices, such as ginger and coriander, require less time and handling but also require human labour. Although they have been harvested for thousands of years, the process of collecting spices hasn't changed significantly — almost all spices are still collected by hand.

using spices

Today, spices are harvested predominantly for use in cooking. However, their essential oils are used in medicine, cosmetics and to add fragrance to perfume. In the past, spices were also used for embalming and fumigating. Spices such as turmeric and saffron are also used to add colour to a dish.

availability and storage

Spices that were once as costly and scarce as gold are now commonly available on supermarket shelves, and in increasing abundance and variety. Although spices may be easy to find, it is worthwhile seeking out a reputable supplier of the best quality spices — the intense aroma and flavour that good-quality spices impart to a dish far outweigh the potential additional cost of purchasing the highest quality goods.

Spices are available whole, or in ground or powdered form. Ground or powdered spices, such as ground coriander and nutmeg, tend to lose their flavour and aroma quickly, so buy in small quantities and store in airtight jars, containers or small plastic bags. Plastic and glass airtight jars and containers are a fine choice — but only provided there is little or no gap between the lid and where the top of the spice sits. The more room for air to be trapped in a jar, the quicker the spice will lose its impact. For this reason, jars and containers will keep spices fresh, but only as long as the jars are kept full.

Plastic zip-locked bags are a good choice for storing spices, as air can be pushed out of the bag before sealing. This lessens the damaging impact that exposure to air has on spices. Similarly, ground spice mixes, such as garam marsala, will only keep for a short time. An additional consideration with spice mixes is that the individual components may become stale at different rates, which may upset the balance of flavour over time.

Where possible, buy small quantities of whole spices and roast (if necessary) and grind them, using a spice grinder, coffee grinder, or a mortar and pestle. You should only grind the amount needed for a particular dish, as ground spices will become stale more quickly than whole spices. Whole spices should be kept in the same conditions as ground spices —although they will keep their potency for much longer. Whether ground or whole, you should store spices in a cool, dark place — away from moisture and potential heat damage — for no longer than 6 months (and less time if already ground). Although you can continue to add spices to dishes once they've become stale they will impart little of the desired flavour and aroma.

berries

clockwise from top left: sumac,

sichuan pepper, allspice, peppercorns, juniper berries

roots and bark

clockwise from top left: galangal, turmeric, ginger, ground turmeric, cinnamon, wasabi powder

seeds

clockwise from top left: mustard seeds,
cardamom, coriander, mace, fenugreek,
cumin, caraway, nutmeg

fruits

clockwise from top left: paprika,

dried chilli, cayenne pepper,

star anise, vanilla, chilli, chilli flakes

whole vs ground spices

Used whole or ground in both sweet and savoury dishes, spices define many classics of world cuisines with their incomparable fragrance and flavour. Whole spices are best used for slowly simmered dishes, as some ground spices can turn bitter after prolonged cooking. Whole spices can also be easily retrieved from a dish before serving, or once the desired flavour has been obtained. Ground spices are used in cooking to integrate into the final dish.

pre-made vs freshly ground spices

Pre-made ground single spices and spice mixes are commonly available in supermarkets however, nothing compares to the result you get from roasting and grinding your own whole spices. The intensity of the aroma and flavour bears little resemblance to the relative blandness of pre-prepared varieties. Once you've prepared your own ground spices, you'll never want to use the supermarket variety again.

dry-frying spices

Dry-frying releases aroma and enhances the flavour of most dried spices. To dry-fry your own spices, heat a heavy-based frying pan over medium–high heat, then add the whole spices to the pan, stirring occasionally until they become aromatic. This will usually take 3–5 minutes, depending on the size and type of spice. Once fragrant, remove the spice from the pan and allow to cool. Ensure you remove the spices before they overcook, as spices that have cooked for too long lose their flavour and aroma and add bitterness to a dish. Roasted spices should be uniformly brown and cooked to the centre — not just on the outside. It is not necessary to add any oil to the pan.

For the best result, each spice should be cooked separately in the frying pan and removed. Spices not only take different times to successfully roast, but also release different aromas — making detection difficult in a crowded pan.

dry-roasting spices

As an alternative to dry-frying spices, you can also dry-roast spices in the oven. First, preheat the oven to 180°C (350°F/Gas 4). Put the spices on a foil-lined baking tray and bake for about 5 minutes, or until the spices become fragrant. As with the dry-frying method, it is usually best to dry-roast spices separately as the size and type of the spice will dictate the time needed to release their aroma, and importantly, their flavour.

grinding spices

Whole spices can be ground in a mortar with a pestle or by using a spice grinder or coffee grinder. If using a coffee grinder, you should ensure that it is thoroughly clean and free of any coffee granules, or better still, keep a coffee grinder specifically for the purpose of grinding spices. Once you've ground spices in a coffee grinder, your coffee will never taste quite the same!

Using a mortar with a pestle to grind spices can allow more control over the coarseness of the final mix. However, grinding your spices to a fine powder in a mortar with a pestle is a much more labour-intensive and time-comsuming process than using an electric-powered spice or coffee grinder. A pestle can also be handy for 'bruising' whole spices such as cardamom pods — as pounding lightly softens the hard outer membrane and allows aroma and flavour to infuse a dish.

getting started

The best way to gain knowledge about spices is to experiment and use them in your cooking. Don't be shy — try new spices and new combinations of classic spices to enhance your dishes.

dry-frying spices

Heat a heavy-based frying pan over medium–high heat. Add one type of **whole spice** — such as coriander or mustard seeds.

Stir the **spices** occasionally — allowing the surface area to heat **evenly** and to prevent burning or over-heating.

The spices are heated through when they are **fragrant** and consistently browned. Mustard seeds will **pop** and become fragrant.

Remove spices from the pan immediately to prevent **over-roasting** and allow to cool before **crushing** or using whole in a dish.

fragrant

heaven scent

Not only do fragrant spices add a warm, moreish flavour
to many a meal, they also add a heavenly aroma to the
kitchen — enticing the senses way before the palate.
Coriander, the great spice that amalgamates flavours in
dishes from around the world, is at the centre of the
fragrant spice world. Dry-fry or dry-roast the seeds and just
a few minutes later the air will fill with a delicate, exotic
scent — enough to fire up the tastebuds. Throw a few
seeds in a dish, crushed or whole, and taste that same
delicate scent throughout the dish. The right amount of a
fragrant spice will ensure the dish is not overwhelmed by
flavour. Fragrant spices tend to complement the flavours
of the dish's hero — be it meat, poultry, fish or tofu —
rather than dominate the dish, and your palate. Fragrant
spices are a perfect friend of food — and offer the nose as
much satisfaction as the mouth!

Related to anise, **caraway** has an aromatic, pungent flavour. It is native to Europe and western Asia, and is available as seeds or in ground form.

A native of southern Europe and the Mediterranean, **coriander** seeds are used whole or ground. Crushed, they form a basis for curry pastes and powder.

21

Indigenous to the east Mediterranean, **cumin** has a hot, pungent taste and is used in many cuisines, particularly North African, Indian, Mexican and Japanese.

Juniper berries are used to flavour gin, game, pork and pâtés. Their flavour is slightly pine scented. Crush the berries lightly before using in cooking.

By far the most expensive spice on earth, **saffron**, the stigmas of saffron crocus, imparts a distinctive aroma and bitter, honey-like flavour. It also colours food yellow.

Turmeric, a mild spice, has a woody aroma and a yellow colour. Related to ginger, **turmeric** is from the underground root of a tropical plant.

caraway and parmesan grissini

makes 40

2 teaspoons **dried yeast**

1 teaspoon **caster (superfine) sugar**

350 g (12 oz/2³/4 cups) **strong flour**

1/2 teaspoon **salt**

2 tablespoons **caraway seeds**

2 tablespoons **olive oil**

1 lightly beaten **egg**, for glazing

50 g (1³/4 oz/1/2 cup) grated **parmesan cheese**, for sprinkling

2 teaspoons **sea salt flakes**, for sprinkling

Dissolve the yeast and sugar in 3 tablespoons of lukewarm water.

Put the flour, salt and 1 tablespoon of caraway seeds into a large bowl. Make a well in the centre, and pour in the yeast mixture, 185 ml (6 fl oz/³/4 cup) of lukewarm water and olive oil. Mix to a soft dough.

Turn out the dough onto a floured surface and knead for 5 minutes, or until smooth and elastic. Return to a lightly oiled bowl, cover and leave to rise in a warm place for 1 hour, or until doubled in size.

Knock back and divide the dough into 40 equal portions. Roll the dough into cigar shapes about 20 cm (8 inches) long. Lay on oiled baking trays. Allow to rise for 15 minutes. Preheat the oven to 200°C (400°F/Gas 6).

Brush with the beaten egg, and sprinkle with the remaining caraway seeds, parmesan and sea salt flakes. Bake for 25–30 minutes, or until crisp and golden.

carrot soup with caraway butter

serves 6

caraway butter

1 tablespoon **caraway seeds**

125 g (4¹/2 oz) **butter**, softened

1 **onion**, chopped

1 **garlic clove**, crushed

750 g (1 lb 10 oz) **carrots**, chopped

1 litre (35 fl oz/4 cups) **vegetable stock**

250 ml (9 fl oz/1 cup) **orange juice**

rye bread, to serve

To make the butter, dry-fry the caraway seeds in a frying pan over medium heat for 3–4 minutes, or until they start to brown and release their aroma. Leave to cool and then grind in a spice grinder or coffee grinder until fine. Beat the butter and caraway together until smooth. Place in a small square of foil, roll into a log and refrigerate for 30 minutes, or until firm.

Put the onion, garlic, carrots, stock and orange juice into a saucepan and bring to the boil. Cover and simmer over a low heat for 25 minutes, or until the carrots are cooked.

Transfer to a blender and blend until smooth. Return to the pan, season to taste and heat through. Cut the butter into 5 mm (¹/4 inch) thick slices.

Spoon the soup into bowls, top each with two slices of the butter and serve with some rye bread.

caraway seed rolls

makes 12

3 teaspoons **dried yeast**

1 teaspoon **caster (superfine) sugar**

500 g (1 lb 2 oz/4 cups) **strong flour**

1 tablespoon **caraway seeds**

250 g (9 oz/1²/3 cups) **wholemeal (whole-wheat) flour**

2 teaspoons **salt**

2 tablespoons **milk**

Stir the yeast, sugar, 50 g (1³/4 oz/heaped ¹/3 cup) of the strong flour and 125 ml (4 fl oz/¹/2 cup) of warm water together until smooth and place in a warm place for 10 minutes, or until frothy.

Lightly pound the caraway seeds using a mortar and pestle to help release their aroma. Sift the remaining strong flour and wholemeal flour into a large bowl. Stir in the salt and work in the frothed yeast mixture, caraway seeds and 250 ml (9 fl oz/ 1 cup) of warm water to form a soft dough. Knead for 10 minutes.

Shape into a round and place in an oiled bowl. Cover with a tea towel (dish towel) and leave to rise in a warm place for 45 minutes, or until doubled in size.

Preheat the oven to 220°C (425°F/Gas 7). Knock back the dough on a lightly floured surface, divide into 12 pieces and roll each one out to a 25 x 2.5 cm (10 x 1 inch) log. Form a horseshoe shape and then loop one end over and through the horseshoe to form a knot. Place on two lightly oiled baking trays, cover loosely with oiled plastic wrap and leave to rise for a further 30 minutes, or until doubled in size.

Brush the rolls with milk and bake for 15–20 minutes, or until risen and hollow sounding when tapped underneath. Cool on a wire rack.

roasted root vegetables with caraway and garlic oil

serves 4

2 bulbs **beetroot**, cut into thick wedges

2 **parsnips**, cut in half lengthways

1 **swede (rutabaga)**, cut into thick wedges

4 **carrots**, cut in half lengthways

1½ tablespoons **caraway seeds**

10 **garlic cloves**, unpeeled

3 tablespoons **olive oil**

2 slices day-old **caraway bread**, crusts removed

2 tablespoons roughly snipped **garlic chives**

Parboil the beetroot for 20 minutes, or until tender, then drain. Preheat the oven to 200°C (400°F/Gas 6).

In a large roasting pan, toss all the vegetables with the caraway seeds, garlic and 2 tablespoons olive oil. Season with salt and pepper. Roast for 30 minutes, then turn the vegetables. Reduce the heat to 180°C (350°F/Gas 4) and roast for a further 30–40 minutes, or until golden.

Meanwhile, brush the bread on both sides lightly with the remaining oil. Place on a baking tray and bake for 30 minutes, turning after 15 minutes, until crisp and golden. Cool, then break into chunky breadcrumbs.

Remove from the oven and serve on a platter sprinkled with the caraway breadcrumbs and garlic chives.

tip If you can't get caraway bread, use plain bread, and increase the caraway seeds to 2 tablespoons.

pork and caraway pilaf

serves 4

2 tablespoons **oil**

400 g (14 oz) diced **lean pork**

1 large **onion**, diced

2 **garlic cloves**, crushed

1 tablespoon **caraway seeds**

300 g (10 1/2 oz/1 1/2 cups) **basmati rice**, rinsed until water runs clear

750 ml (26 fl oz/3 cups) **chicken stock**

125 g (4 1/2 oz/1/2 cup) **plain yoghurt**

2 tablespoons chopped **coriander (cilantro) leaves**

Heat the oil in a large frying pan over medium–high heat. Cook the pork until brown, then remove from the pan.

Add the onion and garlic to the pan and cook for 3–5 minutes, or until the onion has softened. Add the caraway seeds and rice and cook for 2 minutes, stirring frequently, or until the rice is glossy and spices fragrant.

Add the pork, pour in the stock and bring to the boil, then reduce the heat to a simmer. Cover and cook for 15–20 minutes, or until the rice and pork is cooked.

Season to taste and serve topped with a dollop of yoghurt and the coriander.

dukkah with flat bread

serves 6

flat bread

250 g (9 oz/2 cups) **strong flour**

11/2 teaspoons **dried yeast**

1 teaspoon **salt**

1 tablespoon chopped **rosemary**

2 tablespoons **extra virgin olive oil**, plus extra for brushing

dukkah

50 g (13/4 oz/1/3 cup) **white sesame seeds**

2 tablespoons **coriander seeds**

1 tablespoon **cumin seeds**

50 g (13/4oz/1/3 cup) **hazelnuts**, chopped

1 teaspoon **salt**

1/2 teaspoon **ground black pepper**

extra virgin olive oil, to serve

Sift the flour into the bowl of an electric mixer with a dough hook attachment and stir in the yeast, salt and rosemary. Add 125 ml (4 fl oz/1/2 cup) of hot water and the oil and knead on high for 8 minutes, or until the dough is smooth and elastic (add a little extra water, 1 tablespoon at a time, if the dough is dry).

Shape the dough into a ball, place in a lightly oiled bowl, cover and leave to rise in a warm place for 45–60 minutes, or until doubled in size.

Meanwhile, make the dukkah. Heat a frying pan and separately dry-fry the sesame, coriander and cumin seeds and the hazelnuts for 1–2 minutes, or until they brown and start to release their aroma. Allow to cool and then process in a food processor until roughly ground. Transfer to a bowl and season with the salt and pepper.

Knock back the dough and divide into six equal pieces. Roll each piece out on a lightly floured surface to form an oval approximately 20 x 12 cm (8 x 41/2 inches).

Preheat a barbecue grill plate until hot, brush the bread with a little oil and cook for 2 minutes. Brush the top with oil, flip and cook for a further 2 minutes, or until the bread is cooked through. Serve with the dukkah and some extra virgin olive oil, for dipping.

tips This is a traditional spice and nut mix from North Africa. It makes a delicious dip served with bread and olive oil and is also good sprinkled over salads. Stored in an airtight container, the mix will last for several weeks. The dough may be kneaded by hand if you don't have a mixer with a dough hook.

Roll each piece of **dough** out on a lightly floured surface to form an **oval** shape.

Cook the lightly oiled **bread** dough on a hot **grill** for about 2 minutes on each side.

aromatic meatballs in rich tomato ragù

serves 4

3 slices **bread**, crusts removed

125 ml (4 fl oz/1/2 cup) **milk**

4 tablespoons **extra virgin olive oil**

1 **onion**, finely chopped

2 **garlic cloves**, crushed

2 teaspoons chopped **thyme**

1 tablespoon **ground coriander**

375 g (13 oz) **minced (ground) pork**

375 g (13 oz) **minced (ground) beef**

2 tablespoons grated **parmesan cheese**, plus extra to serve

125 ml (4 fl oz/1/2 cup) **dry white wine**

400 g (14 oz) tinned **chopped tomatoes**

2 tablespoons **sun-dried tomato paste (concentrated purée)**

cooked spaghetti, to serve

Put the bread slices into a shallow bowl, add the milk and leave to soak for 5 minutes. Crumble up into breadcrumb-sized pieces.

Heat half the oil in a frying pan over medium heat and fry the onion, garlic, thyme and 2 teaspoons coriander for 6–8 minutes, or until the onion is softened. Remove from the heat and leave to cool.

Mix the combined minced beef and pork, soaked bread, onion mixture, parmesan, and salt and pepper and, using your hands, work together until evenly combined. Using slightly wet hands, shape the mixture into 24 balls.

Heat the remaining oil in a large frying pan and fry the meatballs over a medium heat for 5 minutes, or until browned on all sides. (If the frying pan is small, fry the meatballs in two batches). Add the remaining coriander and cook for 1 minute, or until aromatic.

Add the wine to the frying pan and bring to the boil. Cook for 2 minutes, or until reduced by half. Add the tomatoes, sun-dried tomato paste and some pepper and bring to the boil. Cover and cook for 20 minutes, or until the meatballs are cooked and the sauce has thickened. Serve with spaghetti and top with parmesan cheese.

stir-fried prawns and asparagus with lime and coriander

serves 4

1 kg (2 lb 4 oz) **raw prawns (shrimp)**

2 tablespoons **peanut oil**

3 tablespoons **lime juice**

2 teaspoons **ground coriander** .

200 g (7 oz) **snow peas (mangetout)**, trimmed

175 g (6 oz/1 bunch) **asparagus**, cut into 3 cm (11/4 inch) lengths

4 **spring onions (scallions)**, cut into 3 cm (11/4 inch) lengths

5 cm (2 inch) piece of **ginger**, peeled and julienned

2 teaspoons **cornflour (cornstarch)**

125 ml (4 fl oz/1/2 cup) **chicken stock**

2 tablespoons **coriander (cilantro) leaves**

steamed rice, to serve

Peel and devein the prawns, leaving the tails intact.

Whisk together 1 tablespoon of peanut oil, the lime juice and ground coriander. Put the prawns into a non-metallic bowl, pour over the marinade, cover with plastic wrap and refrigerate for 20 minutes.

Heat the wok over high heat, add the remaining oil and swirl to coat. Drain the prawns, reserving the marinade. Toss the prawns in the wok for 2–3 minutes, or until pink. Remove the prawns from the wok and set aside.

Toss the snow peas, asparagus, spring onions and ginger in the wok for 2 minutes. Reduce the heat to medium. Blend the cornflour with 1 tablespoon of water to form a smooth paste. Add to the wok with the remaining marinade, chicken stock and cornflour mixture. Bring to the boil and boil for 1 minute. Toss in the prawns, and sprinkle with the coriander leaves. Serve with steamed rice.

tip It is important that the marinade boils in order to kill any bacteria present.

falafel with rocket and tahini yoghurt dressing

serves 4

falafel

250 g (9 oz) **dried chickpeas**

1 **onion**, finely chopped

2 **garlic cloves**, crushed

5 large handfuls **parsley**

4 large handfuls **coriander (cilantro) leaves**

2 teaspoons **ground coriander**

1 teaspoon **ground cumin**

1/2 teaspoon **baking powder**

tahini yoghurt dressing

3 tablespoons **Greek-style yoghurt**

1 tablespoon **tahini paste**

1 **garlic clove**, crushed

1 tablespoon **lemon juice**

3 tablespoons **extra virgin olive oil**

vegetable oil, for frying

125 g (41/2 oz) **rocket (arugula) leaves**, to serve

Put the dried chickpeas into a bowl and add enough cold water to cover them by about 12 cm (41/2 inches) and leave to soak overnight.

Drain the chickpeas well and transfer to a food processor. Process until coarsely ground. Add the remaining falafel ingredients and process until smooth and a vibrant green colour. Leave to infuse for 30 minutes.

To make the tahini dressing, put all the ingredients in a bowl and whisk together until smooth. Season to taste and set aside until required.

Using slightly wet hands, shape the falafel mixture into 24 ovals (about the size of an egg). Heat 5 cm (2 inches) vegetable oil in a wok or deep saucepan and fry the falafel in batches for 2–3 minutes, or until dark brown. Drain on paper towel and keep warm in a low oven while cooking the remaining mixture.

Arrange the rocket leaves on serving plates, top with the falafel and drizzle over the tahini dressing. Serve immediately.

rib eye of beef with spice rub, parsnip mash and merlot reduction

serves 4

spice rub

1 tablespoon **olive oil**

1 tablespoon **ground coriander**

2 teaspoons **ground cumin**

2 teaspoons **smoked paprika**

2 teaspoons **soft brown sugar**

1 teaspoon **garlic powder**

1 teaspoon **salt**

1/2 teaspoon **ground black pepper**

merlot reduction

250 ml (9 fl oz/1 cup) **beef stock**

250 ml (9 fl oz/1 cup) **merlot**

1 teaspoon **caster (superfine) sugar**

4 x 280 g (10 oz) **rib eye of beef**, bone on (beef cutlets from a rack)

450 g (1 lb) **parsnips**, peeled and chopped

50 g (1³/4 oz) **butter**

3 tablespoons **thick (double/heavy) cream**

1 tablespoon **olive oil**

Mix all the spice rub ingredients together and rub well into both sides of beef. Cover and allow to rest for 30 minutes.

In a small saucepan, add the stock, merlot and sugar and bring to the boil over a high heat. Reduce the heat to medium and reduce the sauce by a third. Season to taste.

Put the parsnips in a saucepan, cover with water and bring to the boil. Cook for 15 minutes, or until soft. Drain and purée in a food processor with the butter, cream, and salt and pepper, until smooth and creamy.

In a large heavy-based frying pan, heat the olive oil over medium–high heat and sear the beef for 4 minutes on each side for medium–rare, or until cooked to your liking. Remove from the pan and rest for 5 minutes in a warm place.

Spoon a dollop of parsnip purée onto a warmed plate, top with a spiced rib eye and ladle sauce over the beef and around the plate.

roasted eggplant dip

serves 4

1 large **eggplant (aubergine)**

2 teaspoons **ground cumin**

1 **garlic clove**, crushed

juice of 1/2 **lemon**

2 tablespoons **extra virgin olive oil**

2 tablespoons chopped **coriander (cilantro) leaves**

Lebanese (large pitta) bread, to serve

Preheat the oven to 220°C (425°F/Gas 7). Prick the eggplant several times with a fork and put on a baking tray. Bake for 40–50 minutes, or until the skin is wrinkled and the eggplant appears collapsed. Remove from the oven and set aside to cool.

Dry-fry the cumin in a frying pan over medium heat for 1–2 minutes, or until the colour deepens and the cumin gives off its fragrant aroma. Set aside to cool.

Cut open the eggplant, scoop the flesh into a sieve and drain for 5 minutes. Chop the eggplant flesh until finely diced. Put into a bowl and stir in the cumin, garlic, lemon juice, oil, and coriander and season with salt and pepper to taste.

Grill (broil) the Lebanese bread, cut into fingers and serve with the dip.

fragrant dry beef curry

serves 4

curry paste

2 tablespoons **cumin seeds**

2 tablespoons **coriander seeds**

3 **green cardamom pods**

2 teaspoons **white peppercorns**

2 teaspoons grated fresh **ginger**

4 **garlic cloves**, crushed

2 **red onions**, roughly chopped

4 **long red chillies**

2 large handfuls **coriander (cilantro) leaves**, chopped

3 tablespoons **olive oil**

1 kg (2 lb 4 oz) **chuck steak**, cut into 3 cm (1 1/4 inch) pieces

400 g (14 oz) tinned **chopped tomatoes**

2 tablespoons **tomato paste (concentrated purée)**

300 ml (10 1/2 fl oz) **beef stock**

200 g (7 oz) **plain yoghurt**

2 large handfuls **coriander (cilantro) leaves**, chopped

basmati rice, **naan bread** and **pappadams**, to serve

spice it

Dry-fry the **spices** until lightly toasted and **fragrant.**

Stir the **yoghurt** and coriander into the **curry** just before serving.

In a heavy-based saucepan over medium heat, lightly toast the cumin, coriander, cardamom and peppercorns until fragrant. Cool and crush using a mortar and pestle or spice mill.

Blend all the curry paste ingredients in a food processor until a smooth paste forms (you may need to add 2 tablespoons of water). If you are crushing the spices in a mortar and pestle, remove the cardamom pods once the seeds are released.

Heat 2 tablespoons of the oil in a large heavy-based saucepan. Brown the beef in batches over medium heat. Remove from the saucepan.

In the same saucepan, heat the remaining olive oil and fry the curry paste, stirring, for 3 minutes, or until fragrant.

Return the beef to the saucepan and add the chopped tomatoes, tomato paste, and stock. Reduce the heat to low, stir and cover with the lid. Simmer for 1 hour, stirring occasionally.

Remove the lid from the saucepan, stir and simmer for a further 30 minutes, or until the beef is tender and the sauce has reduced by half. Season to taste.

Add the yoghurt and coriander just before serving. Serve with basmati rice, naan bread and pappadams.

cumin, tuna and lemon grass salad

serves 4

2 teaspoons **minced red chilli**

2 **garlic cloves**, crushed

2 teaspoons **ground cumin**

1 teaspoon **ground turmeric**

2 tablespoons **lime juice**

300 g (10 1/2 oz) **tuna steaks**, about 2 cm (3/4 inch) thick

125 ml (4 fl oz/1/2 cup) **peanut oil**

8 **new potatoes**, peeled and halved

2 tablespoons **cumin seeds**, lightly roasted

2 **red Asian shallots**, halved and finely sliced

2 stems **lemon grass**, white part only, trimmed and finely chopped

2 **garlic cloves**, finely chopped

2 small **red chillies**, deseeded and finely chopped

2 **makrut (kaffir lime) leaves**, finely shredded

3 tablespoons **lime juice**, extra

Combine the minced chilli, garlic, cumin, turmeric and lime juice in a small bowl. Place the tuna steaks in a shallow glass or ceramic dish and season with salt and pepper. Spread the marinade over the tuna, coating both sides well. Cover with plastic wrap and refrigerate for 2–4 hours.

Heat the oil in a large frying pan and cook the tuna over a high heat for 3 minutes on each side. Remove the tuna from the pan and set aside to cool slightly, reserving the cooking oil. Cook the potatoes in boiling water until tender.

Combine the cumin seeds, shallots, lemon grass, garlic, chillies and makrut leaves in a large salad bowl. Flake the tuna into small pieces and add to the lemon grass mixture. Add the lime juice, strained reserved warm oil and hot potato halves and toss to combine. Season to taste.

chargrilled vegetable skewers with harissa and yoghurt

makes 8 skewers

harissa

2 teaspoons **cumin seeds**

1/2 teaspoon **caraway seeds**

75 g (21/2 oz) large **red chillies**, chopped

3 **garlic cloves**, chopped

1 teaspoon **sea salt flakes**

50 g (13/4 oz) **tomato paste (concentrated purée)**

4 tablespoons **olive oil**

1 **eggplant (aubergine)**, cut into 2 cm (3/4 inch) cubes

150 g (51/2 oz) **button mushrooms**, stems trimmed and sliced in half

250 g (9 oz) **cherry tomatoes**

1 **zucchini (courgette)**, sliced

125 g (41/2 oz/1/2 cup) **Greek-style yoghurt**

steamed rice and **coriander (cilantro) leaves**, to serve

Soak eight bamboo skewers in water for 20 minutes. Heat a small non-stick frying pan over a medium–high heat and dry-fry the cumin and caraway seeds for 30 seconds, or until fragrant. Place into the bowl of a small food processor with the chillies, garlic, salt, 50 ml (13/4 fl oz) of water and tomato paste. Purée until almost smooth. Gradually add the olive oil and purée until combined.

Preheat a barbecue or chargrill plate to medium–high heat. Thread the eggplant, mushrooms, tomatoes and zucchini onto the skewers. Brush generously with half the harissa.

Cook the skewers for 5–7 minutes on each side, or until golden. Serve the skewers with the extra harissa, yoghurt, steamed rice and garnished with coriander, if desired.

seared beef rice paper rolls

makes 20

11/2 tablespoons **olive oil**

1 **bird's eye chilli**, cut in half, deseeded
and finely chopped

2 **garlic cloves**, crushed

2 teaspoons **ground cumin**

375 g (13 oz) **beef eye fillet**

160 g (53/4 oz/2/3 cup) **Greek-style
yoghurt**

2 tablespoons shredded **mint**

2 tablespoons **lemon juice**

1 large **red capsicum (pepper)**, sliced
into 4 flat sides and trimmed

20 sheets of **rice paper** (19 cm/
71/2 inches square or round)

70 g (21/2 oz) **snow peas (mangetout)**,
trimmed and julienned

1 small **Lebanese (short) cucumber**,
julienned

1 large **carrot**, julienned

1 handful **coriander (cilantro) leaves**

In a small bowl, combine 1 tablespoon of the olive oil, and the chilli, garlic and cumin, and season with salt and pepper. Rub over the fillet, cover with plastic wrap and marinate for 2 hours.

In a small bowl, combine the yoghurt, mint, lemon juice, and season with salt and pepper. Refrigerate until needed. Heat a barbecue grill plate to medium–high heat. Chargrill the capsicum for 4 minutes on each side, or until lightly blackened. Remove from the heat and place in a sealed plastic bag. Allow to cool, peel off the skins and finely slice.

Cook the steak for 5–7 minutes (depending on thickness) on each side until medium–rare, or until cooked to your liking. Cover with foil and set aside to rest before slicing very finely.

Soak a sheet of rice paper in warm water for 30 seconds, or until soft. Lay onto a clean tea towel (dish towel) and fill with a small quantity of capsicum, snow peas, cucumber, carrot, beef and coriander. Drizzle with the minted yoghurt, and fold the rice paper up from the bottom to enclose the filling. Repeat with the remaining rice paper. Serve with extra minted yoghurt.

country-style pork and juniper terrine

serves 12

500 g (1 lb 2 oz) **bacon slices**

500 g (1 lb 2 oz) **pork belly**, diced

500 g (1 lb 2 oz) **lean pork**, diced

1 small **onion**, finely chopped

2 **garlic cloves**, crushed

4 tablespoons **dry white wine**

2 tablespoons **brandy**

1 tablespoon chopped **thyme**

2 tablespoons chopped **parsley**

1/2 teaspoon **ground nutmeg**

8 **juniper berries**, crushed

baguette and **salad leaves**,
    to serve

Cut the eye piece of the bacon slices and set aside. Use the long thin strips of bacon to line the base and sides of a 1 litre (35 fl oz/4 cup) capacity loaf (bar) tin. If any thin strips remain, cut into dice.

Put the pork belly, lean pork and chopped bacon, if any, into a food processor and process briefly until coarsely minced. Transfer to a large bowl and mix in all the remaining ingredients except the baguette and salad leaves until evenly combined. Cover and set aside for 1 hour to allow the flavours to infuse.

Preheat the oven to 150°C (300°F/Gas 2). Spoon the pork mixture into the prepared tin and smooth the top. Arrange the reserved eye bacon pieces over the top and cover the loaf tin with foil. Transfer to a roasting pan. Pour in enough boiling water to come halfway up the sides of the tin, transfer to the oven and cook for 1 hour. Remove the foil and cook for a further 30 minutes, or until a skewer inserted into the centre comes out hot.

Remove the terrine from the oven carefully so as not to spill any meat juices and leave to cool. Remove the tin from the roasting pan. Place a piece of baking paper over the terrine, top with a heavy weight and refrigerate overnight.

Unmould the terrine, wipe or scrape off any excess fat (jelly) and cut into thin slices. Serve with a baguette and salad leaves.

fillets of venison with juniper berries and red wine jus

serves 4

red wine jus

250 ml (9 fl oz/1 cup) good-quality **cabernet sauvignon**

250 ml (9 fl oz/1 cup) **game** or **veal stock**

8 **juniper berries**, crushed

2 **garlic cloves**, bruised

4 sprigs **thyme**, plus extra to serve

50 g (13/4 oz) **butter**, cut into small cubes

20 g (3/4 oz) **butter**

1 tablespoon **olive oil**

2 x 400 g (14 oz) **venison fillets**

mashed potato and **steamed green beans**, to serve

Preheat the oven to 200°C (400°F/Gas 6). Put all the sauce ingredients except the butter in a saucepan over high heat. Bring to the boil and reduce the heat to medium. Cook the liquid for 10–12 minutes, or until reduced by one-third. Strain the liquid through a fine sieve and return to a clean saucepan. Reheat over a low heat, and add cubes of butter one at a time, whisking with a balloon whisk until all the butter is added.

In a roasting pan over high heat, melt the butter and olive oil. Sear the venison fillets until well browned all over. Place in the oven for 15 minutes. Remove from the oven, cover with foil and rest for 10 minutes.

Slice the fillets of venison into 2 cm (3/4 inch) thick pieces. Place onto warm plates and ladle with the red wine jus. Garnish with extra thyme sprigs and serve with creamy mashed potato and green beans.

vodka and juniper cured salmon

serves 6–8

10 **juniper berries**

2 tablespoons **sea salt flakes**

80 g (2¾ oz/1⅓ cups) chopped **dill**

grated zest of 1 **lime**

2 teaspoons **ground black pepper**

3 tablespoons **vodka**

3 teaspoons **caster (superfine) sugar**

500 g (1 lb 2 oz) boneless, skinless
   salmon fillet

mustard and dill sauce

1 tablespoon **dijon mustard**

1 teaspoon **caster (superfine) sugar**

100 ml (3½ fl oz) **sunflower oil**

2 teaspoons **white wine vinegar**

2 tablespoons chopped **dill**

rye bread, to serve

Roughly crush the juniper berries using a mortar and pestle or spice grinder. In a shallow non-metallic dish, combine the salt, dill, juniper, lime zest, pepper, vodka and sugar and spread the mixture evenly in the dish. Lay the salmon in the dish and cover the fish with plastic wrap. Top the salmon with a slightly smaller dish filled with a heavy weight and refrigerate for 2 days, turning the salmon over every 12 hours.

Mix the mustard and sugar together in a bowl and gradually whisk in the oil until combined. Stir in the vinegar, dill and 1 tablespoon of boiling water and season to taste.

Remove the salmon from the marinade. Rinse under cold water to remove excess marinade and pat dry. Using a sharp knife, cut the salmon into thin slices.

Drizzle the salmon with the mustard and dill sauce and serve with rye bread.

lamb with juniper and port sauce

serves 4

500 ml (17 fl oz/2 cups) **chicken stock**

150 g (5½ oz/1 cup) **polenta**

12 French trimmed **lamb cutlets**

1 tablespoon **oil**

185 ml (6 fl oz/¾ cup) **port**

5 **juniper berries**

50 g (1¾ oz) **butter**, cut into cubes

Bring the stock and 375 ml (13 fl oz/1½ cups) of water to the boil in a large saucepan. Add the polenta and stir with a wooden spoon. Cook over a low heat, stirring occasionally, for about 10 minutes, or until smooth and creamy.

Meanwhile, rub each cutlet with oil and salt and pepper. Cook in a heavy-based frying pan over high heat for 2 minutes on each side, or until cooked to your liking. Remove the lamb from the pan and keep warm.

Pour the port and 3 tablespoons of water into the frying pan, stirring with a wooden spoon. Add the juniper berries, reduce the heat and simmer for 5 minutes, or until the liquid has reduced by half. Add the butter, one cube at a time, stirring constantly until all the butter is incorporated.

Serve the lamb with the polenta, drizzled with the sauce.

spiced duck breasts, potato galettes and caramelized pears

serves 4

marinade

1 tablespoon crushed **juniper berries**

1 tablespoon crushed **black peppercorns**

1 tablespoon **honey**

2 tablespoons **cognac**

1/4 teaspoon **ground nutmeg**

2 teaspoons **sea salt flakes**

4 large **duck breasts**, skin on

300 g (101/2 oz) **all-purpose potatoes**

50 g (13/4 oz) **butter**, cut into cubes

1 tablespoon chopped **thyme**

1 tablespoon **olive oil**

70 g (21/2 oz) **butter**, extra

2 firm **pears**

2 teaspoons **caster (superfine) sugar**

2 teaspoons **lemon juice**

400 ml (14 fl oz) **duck** or **game stock**

2 tablespoons **cognac**

Mix all the marinade ingredients together in a shallow non-metallic dish and add the duck breasts. Cover with plastic wrap and refrigerate for up to 8 hours, turning occasionally.

Preheat the oven to 200°C (400°F/Gas 6). Peel and finely slice the potatoes. Line a baking tray with baking paper. Arrange the potato slices, alternating with the finely diced butter, thyme, salt and pepper into four rounds about 8 cm (3¼ inches) in diameter. Bake for 25 minutes, or until crisp and golden on the edges.

Meanwhile, remove the duck from the marinade and pat dry with paper towel. In a large frying pan, heat the olive oil and 20 g (¾ oz) of the extra butter together. Sear the duck breasts, skin side down, over high heat for 3 minutes. Turn over and cook on the other side for 3 minutes. Place on a tray and cook for 6 minutes for medium, or until cooked to your liking.

Peel, core and cut the pears into eighths. Toss in a bowl with the sugar and lemon juice. Discard all but 1 tablespoon of fat from the pan and cook the pears over medium heat for 8–10 minutes, until slightly softened and golden.

In a small saucepan, reduce the stock and cognac by half. Chop the remaining butter into cubes, and whisk into the sauce a little at a time, until glossy. Simmer for a further 3–4 minutes, until syrupy.

Cut each duck breast into six slices. Place a potato galette onto the centre of a warmed serving plate and arrange the duck on top. Drizzle with the sauce and arrange the pears on the side.

tip Duck or game stock is available from good butchers. Alternatively, use chicken stock.

Arrange the **potato** slices, alternating with the butter, **thyme**, salt and pepper, into rounds on the baking paper.

Sear the **duck** breasts skin side down over **high** heat.

pea and asparagus saffron risotto

serves 4

450 g (1 lb) **fresh peas** (in the pod), or 235 g (81/2 oz/11/2 cups) **frozen peas**

175 g (6 oz/1 bunch) **asparagus**

pinch **saffron threads**

2 tablespoons **olive oil**

1 **onion**, finely chopped

440 g (151/2 oz/2 cups) **risotto rice**

1.5 litres (52 fl oz/6 cups) **vegetable stock**

30 g (1 oz) **parmesan cheese**, finely grated

Shell the peas into a heatproof bowl. Trim the woody ends from the asparagus, and cut the stalks into 3 cm (11/4 inch) lengths. Add to the bowl, and cover with boiling water. Stand for 3 minutes, then drain and set aside until needed. Put 3 tablespoons of boiling water into a small bowl, and add the saffron threads. Set aside until required.

Heat the oil in a large, heavy-based saucepan. Add the onion and cook over medium heat for 5 minutes, until soft and transparent. Add the rice and cook, stirring, for 1 minute, until glassy.

Meanwhile, put the stock into a smaller saucepan. Cover and bring to the boil, then reduce the heat to low and keep at a gentle simmer.

Add about 4 tablespoons of the hot stock to the rice, stirring constantly. When it has absorbed into the rice, add another 4 tablespoons of the hot stock. Keep adding stock, stirring between each addition, until the rice is tender and creamy. This will take about 25 minutes. Add the saffron and the liquid about halfway through adding the stock.

About 5 minutes before the rice is ready, add the peas and asparagus to the rice so that they will cook with the last addition of stock. Remove from the heat, and stir in the parmesan. Serve immediately, and top with freshly ground black pepper.

provençal seafood stew with fennel

serves 4

4 tablespoons **extra virgin olive oil**

1 large **onion**, finely chopped

1 bulb **fennel**, trimmed and finely
  chopped

2 **garlic cloves**, chopped

2 sprigs **thyme**

pinch **chilli flakes**

grated zest of 1/2 **orange**

3 tablespoons **Pernod**

400 g (14 oz) tinned **tomatoes**

300 ml (101/2 fl oz) **fish stock**

1/2 teaspoon **saffron threads**

250 g (9 oz) **ling fillet**

250 g (9 oz) **swordfish steak**

12 large **raw prawns (shrimp)**

25 g (1 oz/1/4 cup) pitted **black olives,**
  chopped

2 tablespoons chopped **parsley**

cooked tagliatelle, to serve

Heat the oil in a sauté pan and fry the onion, fennel, garlic, thyme, chilli flakes and orange zest for 5 minutes, or until softened and lightly golden. Add the Pernod, bring to the boil and cook for 2–3 minutes, or until reduced by half.

Stir in the tomatoes, stock and saffron. Bring to the boil, cover and simmer for 30 minutes, or until the sauce is thickened slightly.

Meanwhile, prepare the seafood. Cut the ling and swordfish into large chunks. Peel the prawns and using a small knife, cut down the back of each one, pull out and discard the black intestinal tract and wash well. Pat the prawns dry on paper towel.

Add the seafood to the stew with the olives and parsley, return to the boil and cook for 5–10 minutes, or until the seafood is tender. Season with salt to taste. Rest for 5 minutes and serve the stew with the cooked tagliatelle, tossed with a little olive oil, if desired.

tagliatelle with mushrooms and saffron cream

serves 4

15 g (1/2 oz) **dried porcini mushrooms**

30 g (1 oz) **butter**

250 g (9 oz) **swiss brown mushrooms,** sliced

150 g (51/2 oz) **shiitake mushrooms,** sliced

3 bulb **spring onions (scallions),** sliced

2 **garlic cloves,** crushed

125 ml (4 fl oz/1/2 cup) **dry white wine**

1/2 teaspoon **saffron threads**

1/4 teaspoon **cayenne pepper**

300 ml (101/2 fl oz) **thick (double/heavy) cream**

400 g (14 oz) **fresh tagliatelle**

2 tablespoons roughly snipped **chives**

grated **parmesan cheese,** to serve

Soak the porcini mushrooms in 3 tablespoons of water for 30 minutes. Remove from the liquid and slice, reserving the liquid.

In a large heavy-based frying pan, melt the butter over medium heat until foaming, then add all the mushrooms, spring onions and garlic, stirring, for 5 minutes. Add the white wine, reserved mushroom liquid, saffron threads, cayenne pepper and cream. Reduce the heat to low and simmer for 7 minutes, or until the sauce thickens slightly, stirring occasionally. Season to taste.

In a large saucepan, bring salted water to the boil and cook the pasta for 5–6 minutes, or until *al dente*. Strain the pasta in a colander.

Toss the pasta through the sauce and serve in bowls. Sprinkle each bowl with chopped chives and ground pepper. Serve with parmesan cheese.

scallops with saffron butter and cucumber and dill salad

serves 6 as a starter

saffron butter

200 g (7 oz) **butter**, softened

1/2 teaspoon **saffron threads**

1 tablespoon **lime juice**

salad

2 **Lebanese (short) cucumbers**, peeled

1 tablespoon chopped **dill**

1 tablespoon **lime juice**

2 teaspoons **extra virgin olive oil**

24 **scallops**, roe attached in their shell

Mix together the butter, saffron threads, lime juice and salt and pepper in a bowl. Roll into a thin log, wrap in foil and refrigerate until required.

Peel the cucumber flesh into fine strips lengthways using a vegetable peeler, avoiding the seeds. In a bowl, mix together the cucumber, dill, lime juice, oil and season to taste with salt and pepper.

Place the scallops onto a baking tray and top each one with a thin slice of the saffron butter. Cook under a hot grill (broiler) for 4–5 minutes, or until the butter has melted and the scallops are lightly golden.

Place the cucumber salad onto the centre of each serving plate and arrange the scallops around the salad.

spiced basmati and nut rice

serves 4

small pinch **saffron threads**

250 g (9 oz/1 1/4 cups) **basmati rice**

2 tablespoons **vegetable oil**

2 **cinnamon sticks**

6 **green cardamom pods**, crushed

6 **cloves**

75 g (2 1/2 oz/1/2 cup) **blanched almonds**, toasted

75 g (2 1/2 oz/scant 2/3 cup) **raisins**

1 teaspoon **salt**

2 tablespoons chopped **coriander (cilantro) leaves**

Soak the saffron threads in 3 tablespoons of boiling water until required. Put the rice in a sieve and wash under cold running water until the water runs clear.

Heat the oil in a saucepan, add the spices and fry gently over medium heat for 1–2 minutes, or until they start to release their aroma. Add the rice, nuts and raisins and stir well until all the grains are glossy. Add 500 ml (17 fl oz/2 cups) of cold water and the salt and bring to the boil. Cover and simmer gently over low heat for 15 minutes.

Remove the pan from the heat, remove the lid, and drizzle over the saffron water. Cover and leave to stand for a further 10 minutes. Stir through the coriander and serve.

vegetable pakoras with coriander chutney

serves 4

650 g (1 lb 7 oz) selection of vegetables such as **zucchini (courgette),
red capsicum (pepper), orange sweet potato** and **onion** (about 500 g/
1 lb 2 oz peeled weight)

chickpea batter

125 g (4¹/2 oz/heaped 1 cup) **besan (chickpea flour)**

1 teaspoon **salt**

2 teaspoons **curry powder**

1 teaspoon **ground turmeric**

1 tablespoon **sunflower oil**

1 tablespoon **lemon juice**

coriander chutney

4 large handfuls **coriander (cilantro) leaves**

1 large **green chilli**, deseeded and finely chopped

1 **garlic clove**, crushed

250 g (9 oz/1 cup) **Greek-style yoghurt**

1 tablespoon **lemon juice**

vegetable oil, for deep-frying

Gradually add the **oil,** lemon juice and enough water to make a smooth **batter,** while beating with a balloon whisk.

Carefully slip **bundles** of the batter-coated vegetables into the **hot** oil.

Peel and cut the vegetables into thin strips. Sift the besan into a bowl and stir in the salt, curry powder and turmeric. Make a well in the centre and gradually beat in the oil, lemon juice and 185 ml (6 fl oz/3/4 cup) of water to make a smooth batter with the consistency of thick cream.

To make the chutney, put the coriander, chilli and garlic in a food processor with 2 tablespoons of cold water and process until smooth. Transfer to a bowl and stir in the yoghurt and lemon juice. Season to taste and set aside.

Heat about 5 cm (2 inches) of vegetable oil in a wok or deep saucepan to 180°C (350°F), or until a cube of bread dropped in the oil browns in 15 seconds. Lightly whisk the batter and stir in the vegetables. Carefully slip bundles of batter-coated vegetables into the hot oil and fry in batches for 2–3 minutes, or until golden. Drain on paper towel and keep warm in the oven while cooking the remaining vegetables.

Serve the pakoras with the coriander chutney.

turmeric, ginger and lime chicken on skewers

serves 4

8 boneless, skinless **chicken thigh fillets**

4 **limes**

marinade

250 ml (9 fl oz/1 cup) **coconut milk**

2 teaspoons **ground turmeric**

2 tablespoons finely grated fresh **ginger**

1 tablespoon finely chopped **lemon grass**, white part only

2 **garlic cloves**, crushed

juice of 1 **lime**

1 tablespoon **fish sauce**

2 teaspoons grated **palm sugar (jaggery)**

cooked jasmine rice, to serve

Cut the chicken into 3 cm (1 1/4 inch) cubes. Mix all the marinade ingredients in a non-metallic bowl and add the chicken pieces. Cover and refrigerate for 2 hours. Soak 8 bamboo skewers in cold water for 20 minutes.

Thread the chicken onto the skewers. Cut the limes in half crossways.

Cook the skewers on a barbecue flatplate over medium–high heat for 5 minutes, then turn and cook for a further 5 minutes, or until cooked through. Cook the limes, cut-side down, on the flatplate over medium–high heat for 4–5 minutes, or until caramelized.

Serve the chicken skewers with jasmine rice, along with the limes for squeezing over the chicken.

marinated blue eye wrapped in banana leaves

serves 6

marinade

2 teaspoons **ground turmeric**

2 tablespoons **olive oil**

1 **garlic clove**, crushed

finely grated zest of 1 **lemon**

2 tablespoons **lemon juice**

1/4 teaspoon **cayenne pepper**

6 x 200 g (7 oz) **blue eye fillets** or other firm thick **white fish fillets**

banana leaves, cut into twelve 15 cm (6 inch) squares

green salad and **lemon wedges**, to serve

Mix all the marinade ingredients together in a non-metallic dish. Season with salt and ground pepper. Place the fish fillets into the dish, and cover and refrigerate for 1 hour, turning occasionally.

Remove the fish fillets from the marinade and pat dry with paper towel. Place each fillet onto a square of banana leaf. Top with another leaf and secure with toothpicks.

Cook the wrapped fish on a barbecue grill plate or chargrill pan over medium heat for 8–10 minutes, turning once, or until the fish is cooked — this may depend on thickness of fish fillets. Serve with tossed green salad leaves and lemon wedges.

aromatic vegetable and chickpea curry

serves 4

1 tablespoon **peanut oil**

1 **onion**, chopped

2 **garlic cloves**, crushed

1½ teaspoons **ground cumin**

1 teaspoon **ground turmeric**

1½ teaspoons **ground coriander**

1 **green chilli**, deseeded and chopped

2 **all-purpose potatoes**, chopped into 4 cm (1½ inch) pieces

2 **carrots**, cut into 4 cm (1½ inch) pieces

400 g (14 oz) tinned **chopped tomatoes**

80 g (2¾ oz/½ cup) **frozen peas**

420 g (15 oz) tinned **chickpeas**, drained, rinsed

500 ml (17 fl oz/2 cups) **vegetable stock**

90 g (3¼ oz) **baby English spinach leaves**

saffron and cardamom rice

500 ml (17 fl oz/2 cups) **vegetable stock**

6–8 **saffron threads**

6 **cardamom pods**

400 g (14 oz/2 cups) **basmati rice**

Heat the oil in a saucepan over medium heat. Cook the onion and garlic, stirring, for 3 minutes, or until the onion is transparent. Add the cumin, turmeric, coriander and chilli, and stir until the spices are fragrant. Add the potatoes and carrots to the pan. Cook for 1 minute, stirring to coat in the spice mix. Stir in the tomatoes, peas, chickpeas and vegetable stock. Cover the saucepan with a lid. Cook for 20 minutes, stirring occasionally.

Stir in the spinach leaves and cook until the spinach is wilted. Season the curry with salt and pepper to taste.

To make the rice, bring the stock to the boil in a saucepan. Add the saffron, cardamom and rice. Bring the water back to the boil, reduce the heat to low, cover with a lid and steam the rice for 20 minutes. Remove from the heat. Fluff with a fork and serve with the curry.

turmeric fishcakes on lemon grass skewers

makes 15

6 large **red chillies**, deseeded and chopped

6 **garlic cloves**, chopped

4 **red Asian shallots**, chopped

50 g (1³/4 oz) fresh **turmeric**, peeled and roughly chopped (see tip)

50 g (1³/4 oz) piece fresh **ginger**, peeled and chopped

50 g (1³/4 oz/¹/3 cup) **unsalted peanuts**

1 **tomato**, halved and deseeded

2 teaspoons **ground coriander**

125 ml (4 fl oz/¹/2 cup) **peanut oil**

2 tablespoons grated **palm sugar (jaggery)**

500 g (1 lb 2 oz) **boneless snapper fillet**, roughly chopped

4 **makrut (kaffir lime) leaves**, spines removed, chopped

15 stems **lemon grass**

sweet chilli sauce, to serve

Put the chillies, garlic, shallots, turmeric, ginger, peanuts, tomato, coriander and 125 ml (4 fl oz/¹/2 cup) of water in a food processor and blend to form a coarse paste. Spoon into a heavy-based saucepan and add the oil and palm sugar. Simmer over medium heat for 15–18 minutes, or until the water has evaporated and the paste is a rich golden colour. Set aside to cool completely.

Put the fish pieces, lime leaves, salt and pepper and ¹/2 cup of the turmeric spice paste into the bowl of a food processor. Blend for 1–2 minutes, or until the fish is finely chopped and the mixture is well combined.

Trim each piece of lemon grass to form a 20 cm (8 inch) stick. Mould a heaped tablespoon of the fish mixture around each piece of lemon grass at one end. Cook on a lightly greased preheated barbecue grill plate or chargrill pan for 3 minutes on each side, or until golden brown. Serve immediately with sweet chilli sauce.

tips Substitute 2 teaspoons ground turmeric if fresh is unavailable. These quantities make 1¹/2 cups of turmeric spice paste. Freeze the remainder for later use. Use wooden chopsticks as an alternative to lemon grass, just remember to soak the sticks in water for 20 minutes before assembling to prevent the sticks from burning.

intense

spice with attitude

These are spices with bite — not with tongue-tingling chilli heat, but with intense, punchy aroma and flavour. These spices demand attention. If fragrant spices are delicate, then this collection are tough and unruly. With pungent spices, 'small amounts' are the keywords — unless you like your dishes tasting of the spice and nothing like the ingredients they accompany. Add a little pungency to a recipe, let the flavours infuse the dish, then sample it. There's nothing worse than over-seasoning with an intense ingredient — the balance of the dish is lost.

Although less aromatic than the fragrant spices, this intense collection will still tingle the nose. However, the real attraction with these spices is the flavour punch they deliver to the tastebuds.

Not to be confused with mixed spice, **allspice** is native to the West Indies and tastes like a combination of nutmeg, cinnamon, cloves and black pepper.

Fenugreek are the seed-bearing pods from a western Asian plant. The flavour is enhanced by lightly roasting the seeds. This spice is popular in Indian cuisine.

Available fresh, dried or powdered, **galangal** is a distinctive seasoning used throughout Southeast Asia. This rhizome is similar in taste and appearance to ginger.

The outer lace-like covering of nutmeg, **mace** has a similar but more delicate flavour. Sold as fragments known as blades, mace may also be ground into a powder.

Paprika varies in flavour from hot to mild (also called sweet) depending on the type of peppers used. Paprika comes in plain, Hungarian and Spanish varieties.

A spice used extensively in Lebanese and Turkish cooking, **sumac** is a reddish-purple berry with a fruity but mildly astringent lemony flavour.

lamb kibbeh

serves 6

235 g (8¹/2 oz/1¹/3 cups) **burghul (bulgur)**

500 g (1 lb 2 oz) **minced (ground) lean lamb**

2 **onions**, finely chopped

2 teaspoons **ground allspice**

1 teaspoon **salt**

1 teaspoon **ground black pepper**

1 tablespoon **pine nuts**

4 tablespoons **ghee,** melted

filling

1 tablespoon **ghee**

1 small **onion**, finely chopped

1 teaspoon **ground allspice**

1/2 teaspoon **salt**

1/2 teaspoon **ground black pepper**

1 teaspoon **ground nutmeg**

250 g (9 oz) **minced (ground) lamb**

80 g (2³/4 oz/¹/2 cup) **pine nuts**

green salad, hummus and **Lebanese (large pitta) bread**, to serve

Preheat the oven to 180°C (350°F/Gas 4). Cover the burghul with water in a bowl, and stand for 15 minutes. Drain, then squeeze out as much liquid as possible.

Combine the burghul with the lamb, onion, allspice, and salt and pepper in bowl. Knead the lamb mixture with 100 ml (3¹/2 fl oz) of iced water to make a fine paste.

To make the filling, heat the ghee in a frying pan over medium heat. Add the onion and spices, and cook, stirring, for about 3 minutes, or until the onion is soft. Add the lamb and cook, stirring, for about 5 minutes, or until the mixture has changed colour. Stir in the pine nuts. Cool the mixture slightly before using.

Lightly grease a 30 cm (12 inch) oval baking dish (about a 2 litre/70 fl oz/8-cup capacity). Press half the lamb mixture over the base of the prepared dish, top with the filling, and press the remaining lamb mixture over the top. Using a sharp knife, cut 4 cm (1¹/2 inch) diamonds through the kibbeh. Press a pine nut in the centre of each diamond.

Drizzle the kibbeh with melted ghee, and bake for about 1¹/2 hours, or until cooked through. Cover with foil if over-browning. Serve cut into diamonds, with salad, hummus and Lebanese bread.

spice it

caribbean jerk pork

serves 4

1 tablespoon **ground allspice**

3/4 teaspoon **ground cinnamon**

1/2 teaspoon **ground nutmeg**

1/2 teaspoon **chilli powder**

2 small **red chillies**, finely chopped

2 **garlic cloves**, crushed

4 tablespoons **lime juice**

1 tablespoon **olive oil**

4 **pork loin chops** or **cutlets** (about 185 g/61/2 oz each)

steamed rice and **fruit salsa**, to serve

Put the allspice, cinnamon, nutmeg, chilli powder, chillies, garlic, lime juice and olive oil in a bowl and mix until well combined.

Put the pork in a shallow non-metallic dish and spoon the spice mixture over the top. Spread over both sides of the pork and cover and refrigerate for 4–6 hours to marinate.

Preheat a barbecue chargrill or flatplate to medium–high. Add the pork to the barbecue and reduce the heat to medium. Cook for 3 minutes on each side, or until the pork is just cooked. Transfer to a plate and set aside for 5 minutes to rest.

Serve with rice and a fruit salsa.

beef and vegetable empanadas

makes 25

1 tablespoon **olive oil**

1 small **onion**, finely chopped

2 **garlic cloves**, crushed

1/2 teaspoon freshly cracked **black pepper**

1/4 teaspoon **ground cinnamon**

1/2 teaspoon **ground allspice**

250 g (9 oz) **minced (ground) lean beef**

250 g (9 oz/1 cup) **tomato passata (puréed tomatoes)**

1 small **carrot**, finely diced

1 small **zucchini (courgette)**, finely diced

20 g (3/4 oz) **raisins**

2 teaspoons **cider vinegar**

5 sheets **frozen shortcrust pastry**, thawed

1 **egg**, lightly beaten

vegetable oil, for deep-frying

sour cream, to serve

Heat the oil in a heavy-based frying pan over medium–high heat. Cook the onion, garlic and spices for 2 minutes, or until the onion is soft. Add the minced beef and cook for 5 minutes, or until brown. Stir in the tomato passata, vegetables, raisins and vinegar. Reduce the heat and simmer, covered, for 15 minutes, then remove the lid and continue to simmer until thickened. Set aside and allow to cool.

Cut 25 x 9 cm (3 1/2 inch) rounds from the pastry. Put 1 tablespoon of the beef and vegetable mixture in the centre of each round, and lightly brush the edges with the egg. Fold the pastry over to enclose the filling, press the edges and pinch to seal.

Fill a deep-fryer, large saucepan or wok one-third full with vegetable oil and heat to 180°C (350°F), or until a cube of bread browns in 15 seconds. Fry the empanadas three at a time for 2–3 minutes, or until crisp and brown, then drain on paper towel. Serve with dollops of sour cream.

poached chicken salad with hokkien noodles

serves 4

450 g (1 lb) boneless, skinless **chicken breast fillet**

6 cm (2¹/2 inch) piece fresh **ginger**

6 **whole allspice**

¹/2 teaspoon **coriander seeds**

400 g (14 oz) **hokkien (egg) noodles**

160 g (5³/4 oz) **snake (yard-long) beans**, sliced diagonally lengthways

115 g (4 oz) **baby corn**, cut in half lengthways

100 g (3¹/2 oz) **snow peas (mangetout)**, trimmed and finely shredded lengthways

¹/2 large **green chilli**, deseeded and finely sliced (optional)

1 large handful **mint**

1 handful **coriander (cilantro) leaves**

dressing

2 tablespoons **tamari**

juice of 1 **lime**

1 tablespoon **sesame oil**

2 teaspoons **soft brown sugar**

Pour in enough **water** just to cover the chicken and **spices**.

After the **noodles** have been soaking for a couple of minutes, use a **fork** to gently work them loose.

Put the chicken, ginger, whole allspice and coriander seeds into a saucepan, cover with water, and bring to the boil over medium heat. Reduce the heat, and simmer for 12 minutes, or until the chicken is cooked. Allow to cool slightly, then remove and finely slice the chicken.

Place the noodles into a large heatproof bowl and cover with boiling water. Stand for a few minutes, until the noodles soften slightly, then separate with a fork and drain well.

Put the chicken, beans, corn, snow peas, chilli, mint, coriander and combined dressing ingredients in a bowl, and toss lightly.

Divide the noodles among four serving plates. Top with salad and serve immediately.

lamb tagine with almond couscous

serves 4

4 tablespoons **olive oil**

1 kg (2 lb 4 oz) **diced lamb**

1 **onion**, sliced

2 **garlic cloves**, crushed

2 teaspoons **ground allspice**

1 teaspoon **ground turmeric**

1/2 teaspoon **ground chilli**

2 teaspoons **ground cumin**

1 large **carrot**, chopped coarsely

2 tablespoons **honey**

2 x 5 cm (2 inch) pieces **lemon zest**

2 tablespoons **lemon juice**

375 ml (13 fl oz/11/2 cups) **chicken stock**

85 g (3 oz/1/2 cup) **pitted dried dates**

almond couscous

300 g (101/2 oz/12/3 cups) **couscous**

1 tablespoon **olive oil**

3 tablespoons roughly chopped

  parsley

2 teaspoons finely grated **lemon zest**

40 g (11/2 oz/1/2 cup) **flaked almonds**,

  toasted

Heat half the oil in a large saucepan over high heat. Cook the lamb in batches for about 3–4 minutes, or until browned all over. Remove from heat. Cover and keep warm.

Heat the remaining oil in the same pan over medium heat. Cook the onion, garlic and spices for 5 minutes, or until the onion is soft. Return the meat to the pan, and add the carrot, honey, lemon zest, juice, stock and 125 ml (4 fl oz/1/2 cup) of water. Bring to the boil. Simmer over low heat, covered, for 1 hour, stirring occasionally. Add the dates, cover and simmer over low heat for 30 minutes.

Meanwhile, place the couscous in a heatproof bowl, pour over 375 ml (13 fl oz/ 11/2 cups) of boiling water, and oil and stir for 30 seconds. Cover and stand for 5 minutes. Fluff the couscous with a fork to remove any lumps. Stir in the remaining ingredients. Serve the tagine with the couscous.

pork vindaloo

serves 4

1 kg (2 lb 4 oz) **diced pork**

3 tablespoons **white vinegar**

3 cm (1¼ inch) piece fresh **ginger**, peeled, finely grated

5 **garlic cloves**, crushed

1 tablespoon **ground fenugreek**

2 teaspoons **ground cumin**

1 teaspoon **ground cinnamon**

1 teaspoon **chilli flakes**

½ teaspoon **ground cardamom**

½ teaspoon **ground black pepper**

1 teaspoon **salt**

2 tablespoons **ghee**

1 **onion**, chopped

750 ml (26 fl oz/3 cups) **beef stock**

1 teaspoon **cornflour (cornstarch)**

20 g (¾ oz) **palm sugar (jaggery)**

cooked basmati rice, to serve

Combine the pork, vinegar, ginger, garlic, pepper, salt, and spices in a large bowl and mix well. Cover and refrigerate for 2 hours, or overnight.

Heat the ghee in a large saucepan over medium heat and cook the pork in batches until lightly browned. Add the onion to the same pan and cook, stirring, for about 3 minutes, or until soft. Return the pork to the pan with the stock, and bring to the boil. Season to taste with salt. Reduce the heat to low and cook, covered, for 1 hour 30 minutes, or until the pork is tender.

Combine the cornflour and 1 teaspoon of water in a small jug and add to the pork mixture. Bring to the boil over high heat until the mixture thickens slightly. Stir in the palm sugar until dissolved. Serve the pork vindaloo with basmati rice.

dhal with vegetables

serves 6

150 g (5¹/2 oz/²/3 cup) **yellow lentils**

150 g (5¹/2 oz/scant ²/3 cup) **red lentils**

1 tablespoon **ghee**

1 **onion**, chopped

2 **garlic cloves**, crushed

1 tablespoon **fenugreek seeds**

2 teaspoons **ground cumin**

2 teaspoons **ground coriander**

¹/2 teaspoon **ground turmeric**

400 g (14 oz) tin **chopped tomatoes**

750 ml (26 fl oz/3 cups) **vegetable stock**

2 **carrots**, chopped

250 g (9 oz) **cauliflower florets**

150 g (5¹/2 oz) **green beans**, trimmed and halved

3 tablespoons **cream (whipping)**

2 tablespoons chopped **coriander (cilantro) leaves**

naan bread, to serve

Rinse the lentils, separately, under cold water until the water runs clear, then drain well. Put the yellow lentils in a small bowl, cover with water and stand for 30 minutes, then drain well.

Heat the ghee in a saucepan over medium heat. Cook the onion and garlic, stirring, for about 3 minutes, or until the onion is soft.

Stir in the spices and cook, stirring, for about 30 seconds, or until fragrant. Add the lentils, tomatoes and stock. Bring to the boil over high heat, then reduce the heat to low and simmer, covered, for 20 minutes.

Stir in the carrots and cauliflower. Cover and cook for 10 minutes. Add the beans and cook, covered, for a further 5 minutes, or until the lentils are tender and the vegetables are cooked. Season to taste. Stir in the cream. Serve the dhal sprinkled with the coriander leaves and serve with naan bread.

southern indian seafood curry

serves 4

2 tablespoons **vegetable oil**

1/2 teaspoon **fenugreek seeds**

10 fresh **curry leaves**

2 **green chillies**, split lengthways

1 **red onion**, sliced

1 tablespoon **tamarind concentrate**

1/2 teaspoon **ground turmeric**

1/2 teaspoon **paprika**

1/2 teaspoon **salt**

1/2 teaspoon **ground black pepper**

375 ml (13 fl oz/11/2 cups) **coconut milk**

750 g (1 lb 10 oz) **mixed seafood**, such as **snapper** or **firm white fish fillets**, cut into pieces; **prawns (shrimp)**, peeled and deveined, tails intact; **scallops**; **squid**, sliced into rings

400 g (14 oz) tinned **chopped tomatoes**

Heat the oil in a saucepan, add the fenugreek seeds and cook over medium heat until they pop. Add the curry leaves, chillies and onion and cook for 8 minutes, or until the onion is soft.

Add the tamarind, turmeric, paprika, salt, pepper, and half the coconut milk. Bring to the boil, reduce the heat to a simmer and add the seafood. Cook for 8 minutes, or until it changes colour, turning the seafood during cooking.

Add the tomatoes and the remaining coconut milk. Cover and cook for a further 4 minutes, or until the seafood is tender.

spiced potatoes

serves 6

1.5 kg (3 lb 5 oz) **roasting potatoes**, peeled, cut into 4 cm (1½ inch) pieces

2 tablespoons **ghee**

2 teaspoons **ground fenugreek**

1 **garlic clove**, crushed

1 teaspoon finely grated fresh **ginger**

1 tablespoon **black mustard seeds**

pinch **saffron threads**

80 g (2¾ oz) **baby English spinach leaves**

Preheat the oven to 180°C (350°F/Gas 4). Boil, steam or microwave the potatoes until just tender, then drain well.

Melt the ghee in a small frying pan over medium heat. Cook the fenugreek, garlic, ginger, mustard seeds and saffron. Season with salt and stir, for about 1 minute, or until fragrant.

Place the potatoes in a large roasting pan, add the spice mixture and toss to coat the potatoes. Bake for about 1 hour, or until the potatoes are lightly browned. Remove from the oven, toss the spinach through the potatoes and serve immediately.

butterflied roast chicken in fenugreek and coriander paste

serves 4

2 tablespoons **fenugreek seeds**

1/4 teaspoon **cardamom seeds**

1/4 teaspoon **caraway seeds**

1/4 teaspoon **coriander seeds**

1 small **red chilli**, deseeded and
   chopped

2 tablespoons chopped **garlic**

1 large handful chopped **coriander**
   (cilantro) stems and **leaves**

2 tablespoons **lemon juice**

2 tablespoons **olive oil**

1 teaspoon **salt**

1.6 kg (3 lb 8 oz) **whole chicken**

green salad and **crusty bread**, to serve

Put the fenugreek seeds in a small bowl and cover with cold water. Leave to soak overnight, as this will remove any bitterness from the seed. It will absorb much of the water, swell and become gelatinous. Drain and rinse.

Put the cardamom, caraway and coriander seeds in a dry frying pan and roast over high heat until fragrant. Remove and set aside to cool.

Combine all the ingredients except the chicken, salad and bread with the drained fenugreek seeds and process in a food processor until a paste forms.

To butterfly the chicken, use poultry shears or heavy kitchen scissors to cut down either side of the backbone. Pierce the top of the breast bone from the inside then open out the chicken and press out flat. Rub the paste over the chicken evenly and marinate for at least 2 hours, or vernight.

Preheat the oven to 200°C (400°F/Gas 6). Place the chicken on a rack, breast side up, inside a roasting dish. Bake for 60–70 minutes, turning the bird over halfway. To test if the chicken is cooked, insert a sharp knife or skewer into the thigh; the juices should run clear.

Remove the chicken from the oven and cover with foil, then rest for 10–15 minutes before carving. Serve with a green salad and crusty bread.

fresh seafood salad with green chilli, galangal and lime dressing

serves 4

dressing

4 thin slices of young **galangal**, chopped

1 **long green chilli**, deseeded and finely sliced

1 **garlic clove**, crushed

2 tablespoons **lime juice**

1 tablespoon **rice vinegar**

1 tablespoon **fish sauce**

1 1/2 tablespoons **mirin**

1 teaspoon **sugar**

3 tablespoons **vegetable oil**

seafood salad

250 g (9 oz) piece **sashimi-grade salmon fillet**

250 g (9 oz) **squid tubes**, scored and cut into 5 cm (2 inch) pieces

8 **scallops**, shelled

8 **raw king prawns (shrimp)**, peeled and deveined, tails intact

1 large **avocado**, chopped into dice

150 g (5 1/2 oz) **snow peas (mangetout)**, trimmed and cut lengthways into thin strips

60 g (2 1/4 oz) **bean sprouts**, trimmed

1/2 small **red onion**, finely sliced

150 g (5 1/2 oz) **baby Asian greens**

In a mortar and pestle, pound the galangal until broken down into smaller pieces. Add the green chilli and garlic and pound until a paste forms. Remove and put into a small bowl with the remaining dressing ingredients and whisk until combined.

Heat 2 tablespoons of oil in a large frying pan over medium–high heat. Sear the salmon fillet for 1 minute on each side. Remove, cover and set aside.

In the remaining oil, cook the squid tubes, scallops and prawns separately until cooked. Remove and cover. Drizzle 2 tablespoons of the dressing over the seafood.

Combine the vegetables with the seafood. Break large pieces of the salmon from the fillet, allowing 2–3 pieces per person. Divide the salmon and remaining seafood over the salad ingredients. Drizzle with the remaining dressing.

green curry of duck and baby corn

serves 4–6

green curry paste

1/2 teaspoon **coriander seeds**, roasted

1/4 teaspoon **cumin seeds**, roasted

10 **white peppercorns**

1 tablespoon chopped **green bird's eye chillies**

2 tablespoons **long green chillies**, deseeded and chopped

1 teaspoon **salt**

1 tablespoon chopped fresh **galangal**

2 tablespoons chopped **lemon grass**, white part only

1 tablespoon chopped **coriander (cilantro) root**

1/2 teaspoon **makrut (kaffir lime) zest**

3 tablespoons chopped **red Asian shallots**

2 tablespoons chopped **garlic**

1 teaspoon **roasted shrimp paste**

500 ml (17 fl oz/2 cups) **coconut cream**

3–4 tablespoons **green curry paste**

2 tablespoons **fish sauce**

11/2 tablespoons grated **palm sugar (jaggery)** or **soft brown sugar**

250 ml (9 fl oz/1 cup) **coconut milk**

250 ml (9 fl oz/1 cup) **salt-reduced chicken stock**

1 **Chinese barbecued duck**, chopped into 2 cm (3/4 inch) pieces

125 g (41/2 oz) **baby corn**

2 tablespoons **lime juice**

3 **makrut (kaffir lime) leaves**, torn

2 **long red chillies**, sliced

1 large handful **Thai basil**

steamed jasmine rice, to serve

To make the curry paste, grind the coriander and cumin seeds with the white peppercorns using a mortar and pestle. Set aside. Combine the chillies, salt, galangal and lemon grass in a food processor or mortar and pestle and process until the ingredients have broken down and are beginning to look like a purée. Add the remaining ingredients and the spices. Purée further, adding small amounts of water to loosen the paste. The paste will be coarse, and may not look very green.

Heat a large wok over high heat. Add the coconut cream and fry, stirring all the time, until the coconut cream begins to look curdled as the oil begins to seep out and separate.

Add the 3–4 tablespoons of the prepared curry paste and cook, stirring regularly to prevent it from sticking, for about 3 minutes. The paste will begin to be very fragrant as each ingredient begins to cook. Season with the fish sauce and sugar, and cook for a further 1–2 minutes.

Add the coconut milk and stock, duck and baby corn and bring to the boil. Reduce the heat, simmer for 4–5 minutes and stir in the lime juice.

Just before serving, garnish with the makrut leaves, chillies and Thai basil and serve with steamed jasmine rice

tip Store unused curry paste in an airtight container in the refrigerator for up to 1 week, or in the freezer for up to 2 months.

Purée the **mixture** with a little bit of water to make a coarse **paste**.

Add the **fish** sauce and palm sugar to the **curry** paste and coconut cream mixture.

mussels in galangal and makrut leaf broth

serves 4

6 cm (2¹/2 inch) piece fresh **galangal**, peeled and sliced

1 stem **lemon grass**, white part only, finely sliced

1 kg (2 lb 4 oz) **mussels**, cleaned, beards removed

270 ml (9¹/2 fl oz) **coconut milk**

1¹/2–2 tablespoons **green curry paste**

4 **makrut (kaffir lime) leaves**, finely shredded

1–1¹/2 teaspoons **sugar**, plus extra to taste

3–4 teaspoons **fish sauce**

1 handful **coriander (cilantro) leaves**

1 handful **mint**

Fill a large frying pan with 500 ml (17 fl oz/2 cups) of water and bring to the boil. Add the galangal and the lemon grass to the frying pan and cook for 2 minutes. Add the mussels, cover tightly and cook for 3 minutes, shaking the pan. Discard any mussels that do not open. Reserve 250 ml (9 fl oz/1 cup) of the stock, the galangal and the lemon grass.

In a wok, add the coconut milk and bring to the boil. Add the curry paste, lime leaves and sugar. Stir and simmer for 3 minutes, or until the oil comes to the surface. Add the reserved galangal and lemon grass and simmer for a further 2 minutes. Return the mussels to the wok and stir until the mussels are covered with the sauce. Add the fish sauce and extra sugar, to taste, and reserved stock to adjust flavours and mix well.

In a small bowl, combine the coriander and mint leaves. To serve, divide the mussels among four bowls and top with the fresh herbs.

beef satay

serves 4

650 g (1 lb 7 oz) **rump steak**, finely sliced

lime wedges, to serve

2 tablespoons chopped **coriander (cilantro) leaves**, to serve

satay sauce

2 teaspoons **peanut oil**

1 small **onion**, finely chopped

2 tablespoons chopped **lemon grass**, white part only

2 tablespoons finely grated fresh **galangal**

1 **red bird's eye chilli**, finely chopped

140 g (5 oz) **crunchy peanut butter**

250 ml (9 fl oz/1 cup) **coconut milk**

Soak 12 bamboo skewers in cold water for 20 minutes. Thread the beef evenly onto the skewers.

To make the satay sauce, heat the oil in a small saucepan over medium heat and cook the onion, stirring, for 3 minutes, or until soft. Add the lemon grass, galangal and chilli and cook, stirring, for 1 minute, or until fragrant. Stir in the peanut butter and coconut milk and cook over low heat until well combined and heated through.

Heat an oiled barbecue grill plate or chargrill pan over high heat. Lightly brush the beef with oil. Cook the skewers for about 3 minutes on each side, or until browned and cooked as desired.

Serve the beef with the satay sauce and lime wedges and sprinkle with the coriander.

tom yum gai

serves 4

1.25 litres (44 fl oz/5 cups) good-quality
   chicken stock
4 pieces fresh **galangal** (about 5 cm/
   2 inches long)
4 **makrut (kaffir lime) leaves**, finely
   shredded
1 stem **lemon grass**, white part only,
   thickly sliced
4 tablespoons **lime juice**
3–4 teaspoons **fish sauce**

2 teaspoons **red curry paste**
350 g (12 oz) boneless, skinless **chicken
   thigh fillets**, chopped
1 small **red chilli**, finely sliced
12 **button mushrooms**, cut in half
1 handful **coriander (cilantro) leaves**
1 handful **mint**
3 **spring onions (scallions)**, finely sliced

Bring the stock to the boil in a saucepan over high heat. Add the galangal, makrut leaves and lemon grass and cook for 8 minutes. Reduce the heat and add the lime juice, fish sauce and curry paste. Stir and simmer for a further 2 minutes.

Add the chicken and cook for 8 minutes, or until cooked. Remove and set aside. Adjust the taste with a little extra lime juice and fish sauce, if necessary. Strain the broth through muslin (cheesecloth), and discard the pieces. Return the broth to the saucepan. Add the chilli, mushrooms and chicken pieces.

Serve the soup topped with herb leaves and spring onions.

cavolo nero and ricotta frittata

serves 4

150 g (5¹/2 oz) **cavolo nero**

1 tablespoon **olive oil**

1 small **onion**, finely chopped

2 **garlic cloves**, crushed

200 g (7 oz) fresh **ricotta cheese**

6 **eggs**

¹/2 teaspoon **ground mace**

2 tablespoons finely grated **parmesan cheese**

crusty bread or **thick toast**, to serve

Cut the leaves of the cavolo nero from the stems, wash and dry thoroughly, and roughly chop. Heat the oil in a 26 cm (10¹/2 inch) non-stick frying pan, and cook the onion over medium heat for 5 minutes, or until soft. Add the garlic and cook for a further 1 minute.

Add half the cavolo nero to the pan, and toss until softened slightly, then add the remaining leaves and cook, stirring regularly, until soft and glossy dark green.

Beat the ricotta in a large bowl using electric beaters until smooth, then add the eggs and mace, and beat on low until combined. Don't worry if there are still a few little lumps of ricotta. Stir in the cavolo nero mixture and parmesan, and season with salt and freshly ground black pepper. Transfer the mixture back into the frying pan, and cook over medium–low heat for 8 minutes, or until set underneath.

Cook the top of the frittata under a hot grill (broiler) for 3–4 minutes, until set. (Test by pressing with a fork — the top may appear set but the centre may still be uncooked.) Turn out onto a plate and cut into eight wedges. Serve with crusty bread or thick toast.

tip Cavolo nero is an Italian cabbage. It tastes similar to silverbeet (Swiss chard), which may be substituted.

chicken and winter vegetable pie

serve 6

1 kg (2 lb 4 oz) boneless, skinless **chicken thighs fillets**, cut into 2 cm (3/4 inch) cubes

1 tablespoon **plain (all-purpose) flour**

4 tablespoons **olive oil**

1 large **leek**, finely sliced

2 sticks **celery**, chopped

2 **garlic cloves**, crushed

2 **carrots**, chopped

200 g (7 oz) **pumpkin (winter squash)**, chopped

2 **dried mace blades**

500 ml (17 fl oz/2 cups) **chicken stock**

3 tablespoons **cream (whipping)**

3 tablespoons chopped **parsley**

2 sheets **frozen puff pastry**, thawed

1 **egg**, lightly beaten

Put the chicken and flour in a large plastic bag and shake until the chicken is coated in flour.

Heat half the oil in a large saucepan and cook the chicken over medium heat, in batches, for 5 minutes, or until browned all over.

Heat the remaining oil in the same pan, over medium heat, and cook the leek, celery and garlic for 4 minutes, or until the leek is tender. Return the chicken to the pan with the carrots, pumpkin, mace and stock and bring to the boil. Reduce the heat to low and simmer, uncovered, for 30 minutes. Stir in the cream and parsley.

Preheat the oven to 180°C (350°F/Gas 4). Cut strips of pastry from one sheet, wide enough to fit the rim of a 23 cm (9 inch) pie dish. Press into place, joining where necessary. Cut two pieces from the remaining pastry and join onto the whole sheet, so it is large enough to cover the pie dish.

Spoon the chicken mixture into the pie dish and top with puff pastry, pressing into the pastry rim. Trim the edges and press your finger around the edge of the pastry to seal. Using a sharp knife, cut two steam vents in the top of the pie. Brush the pie with a little egg. Bake in the oven for 30 minutes, or until the pastry is golden brown.

baked fish with mace-infused coconut milk

serves 4

2 x 700 g (1 lb 9 oz) **whole snappers**, cleaned

1 teaspoon freshly cracked **black pepper**

1/2 teaspoon **mild paprika**

1/2 teaspoon **ground turmeric**

270 ml (91/2 fl oz) **coconut milk**

2 pieces **dried mace blade**

1/2 large **green chilli**, split lengthways

1/4 teaspoon **salt**

3–4 teaspoons **lemon juice**

100 g (31/2 oz) **snow peas (mangetout)**, trimmed and shredded lengthways

1 small **red capsicum (pepper)**, shredded lengthways into strips

1 small **yellow capsicum (pepper)**, shredded lengthways into strips

1 handful **basil**

1 handful **coriander (cilantro) leaves**

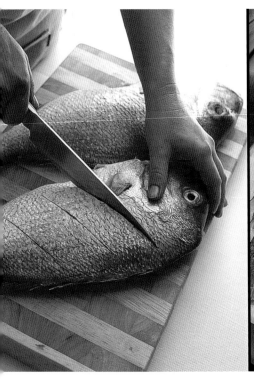 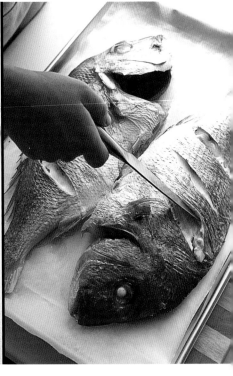

Score the **thickest** part of the flesh to help the **fish** cook evenly.

When cooked, the **flesh** will flake easily away from the **bone** when tested with the tip of a knife.

Preheat the oven to 200°C (400°F/Gas 6). Trim the tail and fins, and score the fish on the thickest part of the flesh with 2–3 insertions on the diagonal to ensure the fish is cooked evenly.

Put the fish on a large roasting tray lined with non-stick baking paper. Bake for 20 minutes, or until the flesh comes away from the bone when tested with the tip of a knife.

In a saucepan, add the pepper, paprika and turmeric and cook over high heat for 1–2 minutes, shaking the saucepan, or until aromatic. Reduce the heat to medium, and add the coconut milk, mace, chilli, and salt. Cook for 4 minutes, or until the oil comes to the surface. Add the lemon juice to taste. Set aside, covered with a lid to keep warm.

In a small bowl, combine the snow peas, capsicum, basil and coriander leaves, and toss lightly.

To serve, carefully place the fish on a serving platter. Discard the mace from the sauce, spoon over the fish, and arrange the salad scattered on top of the fish.

slow-cooked lamb shanks

serves 4

2 tablespoons **olive oil**

8 French trimmed **lamb shanks**

1 **onion**, chopped

2 **garlic cloves**, crushed

3 **dried mace blades** or 1 1/2 teaspoons **ground mace**

2 teaspoons **garam masala**

500 ml (17 fl oz/2 cups) **tomato pasta sauce**

375 ml (13 fl oz/1 1/2 cups) **beef stock**

1 tablespoon **thyme**

mashed potato, to serve

Preheat the oven to 150°C (300°F/Gas 2). Heat the oil in a large roasting pan or flameproof casserole dish and cook the lamb in batches for 5 minutes, or until browned all over. Remove from the pan and set aside. Add the onion and garlic to the pan and cook over medium heat for 3 minutes, or until soft. Stir in the mace and garam masala and cook for 30 seconds, or until fragrant.

Return the lamb to the pan with the pasta sauce and stock and bring to a boil. Cover tightly with a lid or foil.

Roast in the oven, covered, for about 4 hours, turning twice during cooking. Serve the lamb sprinkled with the thyme and accompanied by mashed potato.

chilli tomato pizzas with prawns and scallops

makes 8

1¹/₂ teaspoons **dried yeast**

500 g (1 lb 2 oz/4 cups) **strong flour**

1 teaspoon **sea salt flakes**

1 tablespoon **olive oil**, plus extra
   for greasing

tomato chilli sauce

800 g (1 b 12 oz) tinned **chopped
   tomatoes**

1 **onion**, sliced

2 **garlic cloves**, finely chopped

3 tablespoons **olive oil**

3 teaspoons **oregano**, chopped

1 small **red chilli**, finely sliced

24 **raw king prawns (shrimp)**, peeled
   and deveined, tails intact

24 **scallops**

oil, for brushing

zest of 2 **lemons**

1 teaspoon **ground mace**

100 g (3¹/₂ oz) **rocket (arugula) leaves**

Preheat the oven to 210°C (415°F/Gas 6–7). Put the yeast, flour and salt into the bowl of an electric mixer with a dough hook, and mix well. Add 250 ml (9 fl oz/ 1 cup) of warm water and the oil, and mix on low speed for 5 minutes, or until soft and elastic. Alternatively, knead by hand for 10 minutes. Put the dough into a large lightly oiled bowl and cover. Stand in a warm place for 1 hour, or until doubled in size.

Meanwhile, put the tomatoes, onion, garlic, oil, oregano and chilli into a saucepan. Bring to the boil over high heat. Reduce the heat to low and simmer, uncovered, for 15 minutes, or until the mixture is thick. Season well with salt and pepper.

Lightly knead the dough on a floured surface until smooth. Cut into eight even pieces. Roll each piece into 18 cm (7 inch) diameter rounds. Place onto two large oiled baking trays. Rest for a further 10 minutes.

Spoon the sauce onto the bases. Arrange the prawns and scallops on top, and brush with oil. Sprinkle with the zest and mace. Bake for 15 minutes, or until golden and the seafood is opaque and cooked. Serve topped with the rocket leaves.

roast lamb and chickpea salad

serves 6–8

300 g (10¹/2 oz/1¹/3 cups) **dried
  chickpeas**

2 kg (4 lb 8 oz) **lamb shoulder**

1 tablespoon **olive oil**

3 tablespoons finely sliced **preserved
  lemon zest**

1 **red onion**, chopped

1 **red capsicum (pepper)**, sliced

1 **red bird's eye chilli**, chopped

2 large handfuls **parsley**, chopped

2 tablespoons chopped **coriander
  (cilantro) leaves**

dressing

3 tablespoons **olive oil**

125 ml (4 fl oz/¹/2 cup) **lemon juice**

2 teaspoons **Hungarian sweet paprika**

1 **garlic clove**, crushed

1 teaspoon **caster (superfine) sugar**

Put the chickpeas in a large bowl, cover with water and stand overnight. Preheat the oven to 180°C (350°F/Gas 4).

Drain the chickpeas, place in a large saucepan and cover with water. Cook on a high heat and bring to the boil. Simmer for 20 minutes, or until the chickpeas are tender, then drain.

Meanwhile, place the lamb in a large roasting pan, rub with oil and season with salt and pepper. Roast for 1 hour 30 minutes, or until cooked as desired. Remove from the oven and stand, covered, for 5 minutes. Cut the lamb into large chunks.

To make the dressing, combine all the ingredients in a screw-top jar and shake well. Combine the chickpeas, lamb, lemon, onion, capsicum, chilli, parsley and coriander in a large bowl. Drizzle with the dressing and toss to combine. Serve warm or cold.

creamy chicken and paprika soup

serves 4–6

90 g (31/4 oz) **butter**

1 **onion**, finely chopped

1 stick **celery**, finely chopped

1 small **carrot**, finely chopped

2 tablespoons **Hungarian sweet paprika**

40 g (11/2 oz/1/3 cup) **plain (all-purpose) flour**

2 litres (70 fl oz/8 cups) **chicken stock**

125 ml (4 fl oz/1/2 cup) **cream (whipping)**

300 g (101/2 oz) boneless, skinless cooked **chicken breasts**, finely chopped

crusty bread, to serve

In a large saucepan, melt the butter over medium–high heat. Add the onion, celery and carrot and cook for 5 minutes, or until the vegetables have softened.

Add the paprika and cook for 1 minute, or until the paprika becomes fragrant. Quickly toss in the flour and stir until well combined. Cook for a further 1 minute and remove from the heat.

Add one-third of the stock and mix to a thick paste, stirring out all the lumps. Return the pan to the heat and add the remaining stock. Stir until the soup boils and thickens slightly. Reduce the heat, cover and simmer for 45–50 minutes.

Remove the soup from the heat and stir in the cream and chicken. Season to taste and serve with crusty bread.

spice it

beef goulash

serves 4

1 kg (2 lb 4 oz) **casserole beef (chuck or blade)**, cut into chunks

50 g (13/4 oz) **plain (all-purpose) flour**

11/2 tablespoons **vegetable oil**

1 **red onion**, cut into wedges

2 **garlic cloves**, chopped

800 g (1 lb 12 oz) tinned **chopped tomatoes**

250 ml (9 fl oz/1cup) **beef stock**

1 tablespoon **tomato paste (concentrated purée)**

11/2 tablespoons **Hungarian sweet paprika**

2 **bay leaves**

2 **boiling potatoes**, cut into 1.5 cm (5/8 inch) cubes

3 teaspoons **oregano**, chopped

Coat the beef in flour and shake away any excess. Heat the oil in a large heavy-based saucepan over high heat. Cook the beef in three batches for 2 minutes, or until browned. Add the onion and garlic and cook, stirring, for 2 minutes, or until slightly soft.

Return the beef to the saucepan. Add the chopped tomatoes, beef stock, tomato paste, sweet paprika and bay leaves. Reduce the heat to medium and simmer, covered, for 30 minutes, stirring occasionally. Add the potato, and simmer, covered, for a further 20 minutes, or until the beef and potato are tender. Remove the lid from the saucepan, and simmer for 5 minutes, or until slightly thick. Stir in the oregano and season to taste.

148

bocconcini and semi-dried tomato pizza

serve 4–6

3/4 teaspoon **dried yeast**

1 teaspoon **caster (superfine) sugar**

185 g (61/2 oz/11/2 cups) **plain (all-purpose) flour**

1/2 teaspoon **salt**

1 tablespoon **olive oil**

3 tablespoons **tomato pasta sauce**

4 large **bocconcini (fresh baby mozzarella cheese)**, sliced

120 g (41/4 oz) **semi-dried (sun-blushed) tomatoes**, drained

1/2 teaspoon **sweet smoked paprika**

25 g (1 oz/1/4 cup) shaved **parmesan cheese**

1 small handful **baby basil leaves**

Whisk the yeast, 100 ml (31/2 fl oz) of water and the sugar in a small bowl, then cover and stand in a warm place for 10 minutes, or until the mixture is frothy. Sift the flour and salt in a large bowl, stir in the yeast mixture with the oil and mix to a soft dough. Knead the dough on a floured surface for 10 minutes, or until smooth. Place the dough in a large. lightly oiled bowl. Cover and stand in a warm place for 1 hour, or until the dough doubles in size.

Preheat the oven to 200°C (400°F/Gas 6). Roll the dough out on a floured surface to fit a 30 cm (12 inch) oiled pizza pan. Place the dough in the prepared pan and spread the base with the pasta sauce. Arrange the bocconcini and tomatoes over the base and sprinkle with paprika. Bake in the oven for 15–20 minutes, or until golden and the base is crisp underneath.

Serve the pizza sprinkled with the parmesan and basil leaves.

baked fish fillets with tomato, fennel and olives

serves 4

1 tablespoon **olive oil**

1 **red onion,** finely diced

3 teaspoons **Hungarian sweet paprika**

1 **bay leaf**

100 ml (3 1/2 fl oz) **dry white wine**

300 ml (10 1/2 fl oz) **fish stock**

400 g (14 oz) tinned **chopped tomatoes**

2 **baby fennel bulbs,** finely sliced

4 x 180 g (6 1/2 oz) pieces **perch fillets,** skinned, or other **firm white fillets**

finely grated zest of 1 **lemon**

1 small **baguette,** cut into 8 slices

50 g (1 3/4 oz/1/2 cup) grated **parmesan cheese**

60 g (2 1/4 oz/1/3 cup) **Spanish black olives**

1 small handful **parsley**

spice it

Add the **paprika** and bay leaf to the **onion** and cook for 2 minutes, or until fragrant.

Sprinkle the **parmesan** cheese onto the **toasted** bread slices.

154

Preheat the oven to 180°C (350°F/Gas 4). Heat the oil in a frying pan over medium heat. Add the onion and cook, stirring occasionally, for 6 minutes, or until softened and lightly golden. Add the paprika and bay leaf and cook for 2 minutes, or until fragrant. Stir in the wine and cook for 1 minute. Add the stock and tomatoes, stir and bring to the boil. Reduce the heat and simmer for 15 minutes.

In a 35 cm x 28 cm (14 x 11 1/4 inch) large ceramic baking dish, arrange the fennel to cover the base, then place the fish evenly down the centre of the dish. Pour the tomato sauce over the fish, and sprinkle with half the lemon zest. Bake for 20 minutes, or until the fish is cooked and the fennel is tender.

Lightly toast the bread slices under the grill (broiler), then remove and top evenly with the cheese and grill until the cheese is melted and golden brown.

To serve, carefully remove the fish and fennel onto a serving plate, spoon the sauce over the fish and top with the olives, remaining lemon zest and parsley. Serve with the cheese bread.

roasted tomato and pancetta salad

serves 4

8 **roma (plum) tomatoes**, cut in half lengthways

1 tablespoon **sumac**

2 tablespoons **olive oil**

100 g (3¹/2 oz) sliced **pancetta**

80 g (2³/4 oz) **baby rocket (arugula) leaves**

1 small **red onion**, finely sliced

1 large handful **basil**, torn

3 tablespoons **balsamic vinegar**

2 tablespoons **olive oil**, extra

1 teaspoon **soft brown sugar**

Preheat the oven to 180°C (350°F/Gas 4). Place the tomatoes on a lightly oiled roasting tray, sprinkle with the sumac, season with salt and pepper and drizzle with the oil. Roast in the oven for 30 minutes, or until softened and browned.

Meanwhile, cook the pancetta over medium–high heat in a non-stick frying pan for 3 minutes, or until browned on both sides. Drain on paper towel. Break into pieces.

Combine the tomatoes, pancetta, rocket, onion, and basil in a large bowl. Combine the vinegar, oil, and sugar in a screw-top jar and shake well. Drizzle the dressing over the tomato mixture and toss gently to combine. Serve immediately.

sumac-crusted tuna with saffron rice

serves 4

2 tablespoons **olive oil**

1 tablespoon **sumac**

1 **garlic clove**, crushed

4 x 200 g (7 oz) **tuna steaks**

saffron rice

300 g (10 1/2 oz/1 1/2 cups) **jasmine rice**

pinch **saffron threads**

1 **garlic clove**, crushed

3 tablespoons chopped **coriander (cilantro) leaves**, plus extra whole leaves, to garnish (optional)

Combine the oil, sumac and garlic and brush over the tuna. Season well with salt and pepper. Heat an oiled barbecue grill plate or chargrill pan over medium heat and cook the tuna for 4 minutes on each side, or until cooked as desired.

Meanwhile, combine the rice, 750 ml (26 fl oz/1 1/2 cups) of water, saffron and garlic in a saucepan and bring to the boil over high heat. Reduce the heat to low, cover, and simmer for 15 minutes, stirring occasionally, until the rice is tender. Fluff with a fork. Stir in the chopped coriander.

Serve the tuna on the saffron rice, garnished with coriander.

159

fattoush salad

serves 4

1 **Lebanese (large pitta) bread**, split

2 **baby cos (romaine) lettuces**, torn into bite-sized pieces

2 **tomatoes**, chopped

2 small **Lebanese (short) cucumbers**, chopped

1 **green capsicum (pepper)**, cut into large dice

4 **spring onions (scallions)**, chopped

1 large handful **mint**, roughly chopped

1 large handful **coriander (cilantro) leaves**, roughly chopped

dressing

3 tablespoons **lemon juice**

3 tablespoons **olive oil**

1 tablespoon **sumac**

Preheat the oven to 180°C (350°F/Gas 4). Place the Lebanese bread on a baking tray and bake for 5 minutes, or until golden and crisp. Remove from the oven and cool. Break into 2 cm (3/4 inch) pieces.

To make the dressing, mix the lemon juice, oil and sumac together and season to taste.

In a serving bowl, toss the lettuce, tomatoes, cucumbers, capsicum, spring onions and herbs together. Crumble over the toasted Lebanese bread, drizzle with the dressing and serve immediately.

baked chicken with onions and sumac

serves 4

2 tablespoons **olive oil**

1.5 kg (3 lb 5 oz) **chicken pieces**, skin on, trimmed of fat

5 large **onions**, cut into thin wedges

3 **garlic cloves**, chopped

2 tablespoons **sumac**

11/2 tablespoons **chicken stock** or **water**

Lebanese (large pitta) bread, to serve

green salad, to serve

Preheat the oven to 170°C (325°F/Gas 3). Heat half the oil in a large frying pan over medium–high heat. Cook the chicken, in batches, until all the sides are lightly browned. Remove and set aside.

Add the remaining olive oil to the frying pan and cook the onions for 10 minutes, or until golden. Add the garlic and sumac and cook for 2 minutes. Spoon half of the onion mixture in a deep baking dish, and arrange the chicken pieces on top. Cover with the remaining onion, pour in the chicken stock and cover with foil.

Bake the chicken in the oven for 50–60 minutes. Remove the casserole from the oven and allow to rest for 10 minutes. Season to taste and serve with Lebanese bread and green salad.

barbecue prawns with watermelon and feta salad

serves 4

12 **raw prawns (shrimp)**, peeled and deveined, tails intact

1 tablespoon **olive oil**

2 teaspoons **sumac**

1 kg (2 lb 4 oz) **seedless watermelon**, peeled and cut into 2 cm (3/4 inch) pieces

1/2 small **red onion**, finely sliced

30 g (1 oz/1/4 cup) **pitted black olives**

150 g (51/2 oz) **Danish feta cheese**

1 tablespoon **extra virgin olive oil**

1 tablespoon **lemon juice**

2 tablespoons chopped **mint**

Mix the prawns with the olive oil and 1 teaspoon of sumac and allow to marinate for 15 minutes.

Heat a barbecue flat plate or grill plate to medium–high and cook the prawns in batches for 3–5 minutes, or until golden and cooked through. Remove from heat.

Divide the watermelon, onion, and olives among four large plates. Crumble the feta over the salad in large pieces.

Combine the oil, lemon juice, remaining sumac and mint. Season well and drizzle over the salad. Top with the prawns and serve immediately.

hot

hot hot hot!

Hot spices are more than 'hot' — each has its own distinctive flavour and varying degree of heat intensity. Chillies are hot because they contain capsaicin — a potent chemical that acts directly on the pain receptors in the throat and mouth. The body reacts to the activated receptors by secreting endorphins, which in turn cause a physical 'high' — hence the addictiveness of eating red-hot chillies! If you want to avoid the heat, just remember that capsaicin is primarily found in the ribs and seeds of chillies and that the smallest chillies tend to hold the most heat. Other hot spices can have the same punchy effect as super-charged chillies — from mild tongue-numbing to tear-inducing, nose-clearing agony! For example, mustard seeds and peppercorns can also be extremely potent — both of these spices offer a warm, biting flavour and aroma that blend well with other flavours.

A powder made from ground dried red chilli peppers native to South America, **cayenne** is biting and should only be used sparingly — unless you want a big hit!

There are thousands of varieties of **chilli** plants, with pods an assortment of shapes, sizes and colours, and varying degrees of heat from gentle to painful!

169

There are three main varieties of **mustard seeds**: black, the hottest; brown; and white. Whole seeds have little scent — but mix them with a some liquid and watch out!

Pepper can be black, green or white. These come from the same plant, but are picked at various stages of ripeness. Pepper is sold whole, cracked, ground and pickled.

170

The flavour and fragrance of the Chinese native **sichuan pepper** has a distinctive woody-spicy smell and a strong, hot, numbing aftertaste.

Often compared to horseradish, **wasabi** is, in fact, unrelated. The green root of this Japanese native is available grated, powdered or, most often, in paste form.

cayenne spiced almonds

makes 12/3 cups

11/2 teaspoons **cayenne pepper**

1 teaspoon **ground cumin**

1/2 teaspoon **smoked paprika**

1/2 teaspoon **caster (superfine) sugar**

2 teaspoons **sea salt flakes**

1 tablespoon **olive oil**

250 g (9 oz/12/3 cups) **blanched almonds**

Combine the cayenne, cumin, paprika, sugar and salt in a large bowl and set aside.

Put the oil and almonds in a saucepan over medium heat and stir for 10 minutes, or until golden. Remove with a slotted spoon, add to the spice mix and toss to combine.

Cool to room temperature, tossing occasionally and serve.

spicy seafood gumbo

serves 6

3 tablespoons **olive oil**

30 g (1 oz/1/4 cup) **plain (all-purpose) flour**

1 large **onion**, chopped

2 sticks **celery**, chopped

1 **red capsicum (pepper)**, chopped

2 **bay leaves**

3 **garlic cloves**, crushed

3 teaspoons finely chopped **thyme**

1 1/2 teaspoons **cayenne pepper**

2 teaspoons **sweet smoked paprika**

3 teaspoons **ground cumin**

2 teaspoons **ground oregano**

1 litre (35 fl oz/4 cups) **chicken stock**

400 g (14 oz) tin **chopped tomatoes**

1 tablespoon **tomato paste (concentrated purée)**

350 g (12 oz) **okra**, ends trimmed, thickly sliced

1 kg (2 lb 4 oz) **raw prawns (shrimp)**, peeled and deveined

300 g (10 1/2 oz) large **scallops**, roe and muscle removed

400 g (14 oz) firm **white fish fillets**, cut into 4 cm (1 1/2 inch) pieces

18 **oysters**, shucked

1 tablespoon chopped **flat-leaf (Italian) parsley**

worcestershire sauce, to taste

lemon wedges and **rice**, to serve

Put the oil and flour in a large saucepan over medium–low heat. Stir constantly for about 30 minutes, or until the colour of milk chocolate. Add the onion, celery, capsicum and bay leaves and cook for 15 minutes, or until the onion is softened. Increase the heat to high and add the garlic, thyme, cayenne, paprika, cumin and oregano. Cook for 1 minute, or until fragrant.

Stir in the chicken stock, 375 ml (13 fl oz/1 1/2 cups) of water, tomatoes and tomato paste and bring to the boil. Reduce to a simmer and cook for 1 hour. Add the okra and cook for a further 45 minutes, or until the okra is tender and the sauce is thickened.

Increase the heat to high, add the prawns, scallops, and fish and cook for a further 5–6 minutes, then add the oysters. Cook for a further minute, or until all the seafood is just cooked through.

Stir through the parsley. Season with worcestershire sauce, salt and pepper. Serve with the rice and lemon wedges for squeezing over.

fragrant vegetables with couscous

Serves 4

2 tablespoons **olive oil**

1 large **onion**, chopped

2 **garlic cloves**, crushed

1 tablespoon finely grated fresh **ginger**

2 teaspoons **ground cumin**

2 teaspoons **ground coriander**

1/2 teaspoon **cayenne pepper**

1/2 teaspoon **Hungarian sweet paprika**

400 g (14 oz) tinned **chopped tomatoes**

250 ml (9 fl oz/1 cup) **vegetable stock**

1 **swede**, peeled and cut into 3 cm (11/4 inch) chunks

2 **carrots**, peeled, quartered and cut into 3 cm (11/4 inch) lengths

400 g (14 oz) **orange sweet potato**, peeled and cut into 3 cm (11/4 inch) chunks

2 **zucchini (courgettes)**, cut into 2 cm (3/4 inch) slices

270 g (91/2 oz/11/2 cups) **couscous**

Heat 1 tablespoon of the olive oil in a large heavy-based saucepan. Add the onion and cook over medium heat for 10 minutes, stirring occasionally, or until very soft and golden. Add the garlic, ginger, cumin, coriander, cayenne and paprika and cook, stirring, for 1 minute.

Add the tomatoes and stock, and stir, scraping the bottom of the pan. Add the swede and carrot, cover and bring to the boil. Reduce the heat to low and simmer, covered, for 15 minutes. Add the sweet potato and cook for a further 30 minutes, then add the zucchini. Cook for 15–20 minutes, or until the vegetables are tender. Season to taste.

Put 500 ml (17 fl oz/2 cups) of water and the remaining olive oil into a saucepan, cover and bring to the boil. Add the couscous, turn off the heat and stand for 5 minutes. Uncover and fluff up the grains with a fork. To serve, divide the couscous between warmed serving bowls, and top with the vegetables and their liquid.

fiery barbecue lamb salad

serves 4

600 g (1 lb 5 oz) **butternut pumpkin (squash),** peeled and cut into 3 cm (1 1/4 inch) wedges

1 **garlic bulb**

3 tablespoons **olive oil**

2 x 200 g (7 oz) **lamb backstraps** or **loin fillets**

100 g (3 1/2 oz) **baby English spinach leaves**

95 g (3 1/4 oz) **pitted green olives**

80 g (2 3/4 oz) **goat's cheese,** crumbled

3 tablespoons **olive oil**

1 tablespoon **lemon juice**

spice mix

2 teaspoons **cayenne pepper**

2 teaspoons **mild paprika**

1 teaspoon **mustard powder**

1 teaspoon **ground coriander**

1 teaspoon **salt**

1/4 teaspoon freshly cracked **black pepper**

1/2 teaspoon **ground cumin**

1 teaspoon **dried thyme**

1 teaspoon **soft brown sugar**

Preheat the oven to 190°C (375°F/Gas 5). Put the pumpkin and garlic bulb onto a roasting pan lined with baking paper, drizzle with 1 tablespoon of the olive oil and season with salt and pepper. Bake for 45–50 minutes, or until the garlic is soft and the pumpkin is soft and golden.

In a small bowl, combine the ingredients for the spice mix. Lightly coat the lamb with 1 tablespoon of the mix, reserving the remainder in an airtight container for future use.

Heat a barbecue grill plate or chargrill pan over medium–high heat. Drizzle the lamb with 1 tablespoon of oil and cook for 2–3 minutes on each side for medium–rare, or until cooked to your liking. Cover with foil and set aside to rest for 5 minutes before slicing.

Slice the end off the garlic bulb and squeeze the garlic flesh into a food processor. Purée with half the oil until smooth. Add the remaining oil and purée again until combined. Stir in the lemon juice and 1 tablespoon of hot water and season to taste.

In a large bowl, toss the spinach, pumpkin, lamb, olives, goat's cheese and dressing together. Divide among four plates and serve immediately.

Put the **pumpkin** and garlic on a baking tray lined with baking paper, and drizzle with **oil**.

Sprinkle the **spice** mix onto the **lamb**, then use your fingertips to rub in.

cayenne chicken pieces

serves 6

500 ml (17 fl oz/2 cups) **buttermilk**

3 **garlic cloves**, crushed

1 tablespoon finely chopped **thyme**

1 teaspoon **salt**

2 kg (4 lb 8 oz) **chicken pieces**, skin on (about 12 assorted pieces)

peanut oil, for deep-frying

250 g (9 oz/2 cups) **plain (all-purpose) flour**

1 tablespoon **Hungarian sweet paprika**

1¹/2 tablespoons **cayenne pepper**

1 tablespoon **celery salt**

2 tablespoons **onion powder**

lemon wedges, to serve (optional)

Combine the buttermilk, garlic, thyme and salt in a large bowl. Add the chicken pieces and stir to coat. Cover tightly with plastic wrap and refrigerate for 24 hours, stirring occasionally.

Fill a deep-fryer or large heavy-based saucepan one-third full with peanut oil and heat to 170°C (325°F), or until a cube of bread dropped in the oil browns in 20 seconds. Combine the flour, paprika, cayenne, celery salt and onion powder. Lift the chicken out of the buttermilk but don't shake off the excess. Roll in the flour mixture until thickly coated.

Deep-fry the chicken pieces, a few at a time, for 10–12 minutes, or until deep golden and just cooked through. Drain well on paper towel and rest in a warm oven while cooking the remaining chicken. Serve with lemon wedges, if desired.

chile con queso

serves 6–8

30 g (1 oz) **butter**

1/2 **red onion**, finely chopped

2 **long green chillies**, deseeded and finely chopped

2 small **red chillies**, deseeded and finely chopped

1 **garlic clove**, crushed

1/2 teaspoon **Hungarian sweet paprika**

11/2 tablespoons **Mexican beer**

125 g (41/2 oz/1/2 cup) **sour cream**

200 g (7 oz) **cheddar cheese**, grated

1 tablespoon chopped **coriander (cilantro) leaves**

1 tablespoon sliced **jalapeños in vinegar**, drained and finely chopped

corn chips or **tortilla chips**, to serve

Melt the butter in a saucepan over medium heat. Add the onion and green and red chillies and cook for 5 minutes, or until softened. Increase the heat to high, add the garlic and paprika, and cook for 1 minute, or until fragrant.

Add the beer, bring to the boil and cook until almost evaporated. Reduce the heat to low and add the sour cream, stirring until smooth. Add the cheese and stir until the cheese is just melted and the mixture is smooth. Remove from the heat, stir through the coriander and jalapeño, and season to taste. Serve with corn or tortilla chips for dipping.

spice it

pasta with fresh chilli and herbs

serves 4

500 g (1 lb 2 oz) **pasta**, such as **fettucine**

125 ml (4 fl oz/1/2 cup) **olive oil**

5 **garlic cloves**, very finely chopped

3–4 small **red chillies**, deseeded and very finely sliced

4 **anchovies**, very finely chopped

1 large handful **flat-leaf (Italian) parsley**, roughly chopped

1 small handful **oregano**, finely chopped

1 small handful **basil**, chopped

2 tablespoons **lemon juice**

shaved **parmesan cheese**, to serve

Bring a large saucepan of salted water to the boil. Cook the pasta according to packet instructions until *al dente*, then drain.

Meanwhile, place the olive oil, garlic, chilli and anchovies in a small saucepan over low heat and cook, stirring, for 10 minutes, or until the garlic is lightly golden. Remove from the heat.

Add the oil mixture to the drained pasta with the parsley, oregano, basil and lemon juice. Toss to combine. Season to taste and serve with shaved parmesan.

slow-cooked chilli beef

serves 6

2 tablespoons **olive oil**

1 large **onion**, finely chopped

1 **green capsicum (pepper)**, chopped

2 **garlic cloves**, crushed

2 teaspoons **chilli powder**

2 teaspoons **ground cumin**

1 teaspoon **oregano**

1 kg (2 lb 4 oz) **chuck steak**, trimmed and cut into 1 cm (1/2 inch) cubes

700 g (1 lb 9 oz) **tomato passata (puréed tomatoes)**

250 ml (9 fl oz/1 cup) **beef stock**

400 g (14 oz) tin **red kidney beans**, drained and rinsed

steamed long-grain white or **brown rice, sour cream** and **coriander (cilantro)
    leaves**, to serve

Heat the oil in a large heavy-based saucepan over medium heat. Add the onion, capsicum and garlic. Cook, uncovered, stirring occasionally, for 8–10 minutes, or until the onion softens. Add the chilli powder, cumin and oregano. Cook, stirring, for 2 minutes.

Increase the heat to high and add the beef. Cook, turning often, for 4–5 minutes, or until the beef changes colour. Pour in the tomato passata and stock. Cover and bring to a simmer. Simmer, uncovered, for 2 hours, stirring occasionally.

Stir the beans into the chilli. Cover and cook for a further 30 minutes, or until the beef is very tender. Top with sour cream and coriander and serve with rice.

steamed snapper fillets with chilli and garlic oil

serves 4

4 x 200 g (7 oz) **snapper fillets**, skin removed

3 tablespoons **vegetable oil**

1 tablespoon **peanut oil**

1 teaspoon **toasted sesame oil**

5 **garlic cloves**, very finely sliced

3 small **red chillies**, deseeded and finely sliced

1/2 teaspoon **sea salt flakes**

1 teaspoon finely grated fresh **ginger**

steamed Asian greens and **rice**, to serve

Bring a large saucepan or wok of water to the boil. Line a large bamboo steamer basket with baking paper and punch with holes. Put the snapper fillets over the top then cover with a lid. Put the steamer basket over the top of the boiling water, ensuring it fits snugly on the rim of the pan or wok. Cook for 7 minutes, or until the fish is opaque and flakes easily with a fork.

Meanwhile, put the vegetable, peanut and sesame oils in a small saucepan over a low heat. Add the garlic, chilli and the sea salt flakes and cook, stirring occasionally, for 8 minutes, or until lightly golden. Add the ginger and cook for a further 30 seconds, or until fragrant. Drizzle the oil over the fish and serve with steamed Asian greens and steamed rice

braised pork belly with chilli, ginger and pineapple rice

serves 4

3 tablespoons **dry sherry**

2 tablespoons **olive oil**

2 teaspoons **chilli flakes**

1/2 teaspoon **ground allspice**

1/2 teaspoon **ground coriander**

1/4 teaspoon **ground cinnamon**

2 tablespoons grated **palm sugar (jaggery)**

1/2 teaspoon **salt**

2 kg (4 lb 8 oz) **pork belly** in 1 piece, skin removed

1 tablespoon **rice vinegar**

1 tablespoon grated fresh **ginger**

250 ml (9 fl oz/1 cup) **beef stock**

200 g (7 oz/1 cup) **jasmine rice**

2 **long red chillies**, deseeded and finely diced

100 g (31/2 oz) **pineapple**, finely diced

2 large handfuls **coriander (cilantro) leaves**, chopped

Combine the sherry, 1 tablespoon of olive oil, spices, sugar and salt. Rub all over the pork, cover with plastic wrap and rest for 20 minutes.

Remove the pork from the marinade, reserving the marinade. In a large cast-iron casserole dish, heat the remaining 1 tablespoon of olive oil over high heat and brown the pork all over. Reduce the heat to low and add the reserved marinade, rice vinegar, ginger and stock. Cover with a lid and cook for 2 hours, stirring occasionally, or until the sauce becomes thick and syrupy and the pork very tender. Cook the rice according to the packet instructions.

Remove the pork from the pan and cut into thick slices. Using a metal spoon, remove any fat from the top of the pan juices and pour the sauce over the sliced pork. Mix the chilli, pineapple and coriander leaves through the rice and serve with the pork.

chargrilled mustard-marinated chicken

serves 4

4 boneless, skinless **chicken breasts**, tenderloins removed

marinade

5 cm (2 inch) piece fresh **ginger**, finely diced

2 **garlic cloves**, crushed

3 tablespoons **dijon mustard**

1½ tablespoons **soy sauce**

1 tablespoon **honey**

1 tablespoon **Chinese rice wine**

1 teaspoon **sesame oil**

2 tablespoons chopped **coriander (cilantro) leaves**

1 tablespoon **vegetable oil**

green salad, to serve

Make incisions diagonally into the chicken with a knife, about 2.5 cm (1 inch) apart.

Combine the marinade ingredients and rub liberally over the chicken breasts. Place in a bowl and cover. Refrigerate for at least 2 hours.

Heat a barbecue flat plate or grill plate to medium heat. Brush the flat plate or grill with the oil. Cook the chicken for 7 minutes on each side, or until cooked through and a little charred. Brush the chicken with marinade as it cooks. The chicken is ready when firm to the touch. Serve with a green salad.

195

rack of lamb with mustard crust and roasted vegetables

serves 4

4 tablespoons **olive oil**

1/2 **onion**, finely diced

1 **garlic clove**, finely chopped

50 g (13/4 oz/1/2 cup) **dry breadcrumbs**

1 teaspoon chopped **sage**

1 tablespoon **dijon mustard**

1 tablespoon **seeded mustard**

1 **egg yolk**

11/2 teaspoons **salt**

2 **lamb racks**, trimmed, each with 6 cutlets

12 **garlic cloves**, unpeeled

2 **carrots**, sliced diagonally

1 **red capsicum (pepper)**, cut into thick strips

1 **red onion**, cut into 8 wedges

2 **zucchini (courgettes)**, sliced diagonally

175 g (6 oz/1 bunch) **asparagus**, cut in half, diagonally

1 tablespoon **balsamic vinegar**

Press the breadcrumb **mixture** over the top side of the **lamb** to form a thick crust.

Slice the lamb **racks** into **cutlets** to serve.

Place a small heavy-based saucepan on medium heat and add 1 tablespoon of the oil with the onion and garlic. Sauté for about 2 minutes, or until softened. Remove from the heat, place into a bowl and cool slightly. Combine with the breadcrumbs, sage, mustards, egg yolk, and season with salt.

Spread this mixture across the rack of lamb to form a thick crust. Refrigerate until ready to use.

Preheat the oven to 200°C (400°F/Gas 6). Place the lamb onto a baking tray.

Put 2 tablespoons of oil, the garlic, vegetables and 1 teaspoon of salt in a baking dish and toss well to coat.

Place both the trays into the oven for 30–40 minutes. Stir the vegetables every 10 minutes. The lamb is ready when the crust is golden and the lamb is firm to touch.

Remove the lamb and rest for 10 minutes. Reserve the pan juices. Leave the vegetables in for a further 10 minutes, or until golden. Heat the lamb pan juices with the balsamic vinegar, remaining olive oil and a pinch of salt. Slice the lamb and serve with the roasted vegetables and sauce.

beef with mustard seed butter

serves 4

mustard seed butter

1 tablespoon **vegetable oil**

1 tablespoon **mustard seeds**

1 **garlic clove**, crushed

1/2 **onion**, diced

1/2 teaspoon **Hungarian paprika**

1/2 teaspoon **salt**

2 tablespoons chopped **parsley**

2 teaspoons **seeded mustard**

90 g (31/4 oz) **butter**, softened

marinade

2 **garlic cloves**, crushed

30 ml (1 fl oz) **oyster sauce**

1–2 tablespoons **worcestershire sauce**

1 tablespoon **balsamic vinegar**

1 tablespoon **tomato sauce (ketchup)**

4 x 200 g (7 oz) **sirloin steaks**

green salad, to serve

To make the mustard seed butter, heat the oil in a small heavy-based saucepan and add the mustard seeds. Heat for about 1 minute, or until they start to crackle. Add the garlic and onion and stir for about 5 minutes, or until softened and transparent. Cool slightly, then add to a bowl with the remaining ingredients and combine well.

Place the butter mixture onto a rectangle of foil in a long sausage shape about 2 cm (3/4 inch) in diameter. Roll the foil around the butter, twisting the ends, then refrigerate.

To make the marinade, combine the garlic, oyster sauce, worcestershire, balsamic vinegar and tomato sauce in a non-metallic dish. Add the steaks, cover and marinate for at least 2 hours.

Barbecue or chargrill the steaks for 4 minutes on each side for medium, or until cooked to your liking. Serve topped with a slice of mustard seed butter and a green salad.

indian cauliflower with mustard seeds

serves 6 as a side

4 tablespoons **vegetable oil**

1 tablespoon **cumin seeds**

1 tablespoon **mustard seeds**

1 teaspoon **chilli powder**

1 teaspoon **ground turmeric**

1/2 teaspoon **salt**

1 kg (2 lb 4 oz) **cauliflower**, cut into small florets

90 g (31/4 oz/1/3 cup) **Greek-style yoghurt**

juice of 1/2 **lemon**

7 large handfuls **coriander (cilantro) leaves**

Heat the oil in a large wok over medium–high heat. Add the cumin seeds and mustard seeds. Cook, tossing, for 1 minute, or until the mustard seeds start to pop. Stir in the chilli powder, turmeric and salt.

Add the cauliflower florets to the wok and toss to coat in the spice mix. Cover and reduce the heat to medium. Cook for 10 minutes, tossing about every 2 minutes, or until the cauliflower is tender. Remove from the heat.

Add the yoghurt and lemon juice to the wok. Toss to coat. Toss in the coriander and serve immediately.

deep-fried pork dumplings with hot mustard dipping sauce

serves 4–6

300 g (10½ oz) **minced (ground) pork**

4 **spring onions (scallions)**, finely sliced

1 tablespoon **yellow mustard seeds**

2 tablespoons **light soy sauce**

8 **water chestnuts**, chopped

1 **egg**, well beaten

30 square or round **gow gee (egg) dumpling wrappers**

3 tablespoons **English mustard**

oil, for deep-frying

Combine the minced pork, scallions, mustard seeds, soy, water chestnuts and beaten egg in a bowl. Mix well to combine.

Lay a gow gee wrapper on a dry, flat surface and brush the edges with water. Spoon 2 teaspoons of the pork mixture in the middle of the wrapper. Fold over to enclose the filling in a triangular or semi-circular shape. Pinch the edges together firmly to seal, making sure to expel as much air as possible. Use your fingers to make three or four small pleats in either side to gather the dough around the filling. Repeat with the remaining ingredients.

To make the sauce, put the mustard into a bowl and add 4 tablespoons of water gradually, stirring until smooth.

Heat the oil in a wok and deep-fry the dumplings in batches for 1–2 minutes, or until golden brown and the filling is cooked through. Drain on paper towel. Serve hot with the dipping sauce.

spice it

salt and pepper squid

serves 4

500 g (1 lb 2 oz) cleaned **squid tubes**

2 tablespoons **lemon juice**

2 **garlic cloves**, finely chopped

95 g (31/4 oz/1/2 cup) **potato flour**

1 tablespoon **sichuan peppercorns**, toasted and ground

1 tablespoon **ground black pepper**

11/2 teaspoons **ground white pepper**

11/2 tablespoons **sea salt flakes**, crushed

1 teaspoon **caster (superfine) sugar**

peanut oil, for deep-frying

lemon wedges, to serve

Cut the squid tubes in half lengthways then lay flat on the bench with the inside facing up. Score a shallow criss-cross pattern over this side only. Cut into 5 x 3 cm (2 x 11/4 inch) rectangles.

Combine the lemon juice and garlic, then add the squid and toss to coat. Refrigerate for 1 hour, then drain off the marinade and discard. Combine the potato flour, peppers, salt and sugar and set aside.

Fill a deep-fryer or large heavy-based saucepan one-third full with the oil and heat to 180°C (350°F), or until a cube of bread dropped in the oil browns in 15 seconds.

Coat the squid in the flour mixture, pressing lightly into it to help adhere. Deep-fry the squid pieces in batches for 11/2–2 minutes, or until lightly golden and curled. Drain well on paper towel and serve with lemon wedges.

three pepper steak

serves 4

2 teaspoons freshly cracked
  black pepper

2 teaspoons freshly cracked
  white pepper

1 teaspoon lightly crushed **sea salt
  flakes**

4 x 200 g (7 oz) **eye fillet steaks**

1 tablespoon **olive oil**

40 g (1 1/2 oz) **butter**

2 large **French shallots**, finely chopped

1 **garlic clove**, crushed

2 tablespoons **brandy**

160 ml (5 1/4 fl oz/2/3 cup) **beef stock**

4 tablespoons **cream (whipping)**

1 1/2 tablespoons **green peppercorns
  in brine**, drained and lightly crushed

2 teaspoons finely chopped **flat-leaf
  (Italian) parsley**

steamed asparagus, beans and **new
  potatoes**, to serve

Combine the black and white pepper with the sea salt flakes. Coat the steaks in the pepper mixture, patting on to help adhere.

Heat the olive oil in a large heavy-based frying pan over high heat. Add the steaks and cook for 3–4 minutes on each side for medium–rare, or until cooked to your liking. Remove from the pan and cover to keep warm while you make the sauce.

Reduce the heat to medium and add the butter, French shallots and garlic to the frying pan and cook for 1 minute, or until softened. Remove from the heat and carefully add the brandy, then place back on the heat. Bring to the boil, then add the beef stock, cream and green peppercorns and allow to come back to the boil. Cook for 4 minutes, or until glossy and thickened slightly, adding any resting juices from the steak. Add the parsley and season to taste. Serve the sauce over the steaks. Serve with the asparagus, beans and potatoes.

hot and sour tofu soup

serves 4

4 small **dried Chinese mushrooms**

2 teaspoons **vegetable oil**

1 teaspoon **sesame oil**

3 **spring onions (scallions)**, white part chopped, greens reserved

2 **garlic cloves**, crushed

2 teaspoons finely grated fresh **ginger**

1³/4 teaspoons **ground white pepper**

300 g (10¹/2 oz) **minced (ground) pork** or **chicken**

1.5 litres (52 fl oz/6 cups) salt-reduced **chicken stock**

50 g (1³/4 oz) drained sliced **bamboo shoots**, cut into thin strips

40 g (1¹/2 oz/1/4 cup) drained sliced **water chestnuts**, cut into thin strips

4 tablespoons **rice vinegar**

1 tablespoon **soy sauce**

1¹/2 teaspoons **chilli garlic sauce**

1 teaspoon **caster (superfine) sugar**

300 g (10¹/2 oz) **firm tofu**, cut into 1.5 cm (5/8 inch) dice

1 teaspoon **cornflour (cornstarch)**

2 **eggs**, lightly beaten

Soak the mushrooms in hot water for 30 minutes. Drain, reserving 2 tablespoons of the soaking liquid. Discard the mushroom stems and finely slice the caps. Set aside.

Heat the vegetable and sesame oil in a wok over medium–high heat. Add the white part of the spring onions, the garlic, ginger and white pepper and stir-fry for 1 minute, or until fragrant. Add the minced pork or chicken and stir-fry, breaking up any lumps, for 3–4 minutes or until it changes colour. Add the chicken stock, reserved mushrooms, bamboo shoots, and water chestnuts and bring to the boil. Reduce to a simmer and cook, skimming the surface occasionally, for 30 minutes, or until the mince is tender.

Add the vinegar, soy, chilli garlic sauce, sugar, and tofu. Combine the cornflour with the reserved mushroom soaking liquid until smooth. Stir into the soup and cook for 2 minutes, or until thickened slightly.

Drizzle the beaten eggs onto the top of the soup and leave for 1 minute without stirring, then stir through just before serving. Shred the reserved spring onion greens and use to garnish.

Stir-fry the **minced** pork or chicken until it changes **colour**. Break up any lumps as it cooks.

Drizzle the beaten **eggs** onto the **soup**. Leave for 1 minute without stirring.

213

eye fillet with green peppercorn sauce

serves 4

400 g (14 oz/2 bunches) **cherry
   tomatoes** on their truss
2 tablespoons **olive oil**
3 **all-purpose potatoes**, peeled and
   chopped
1 small **bulb celeriac**, peeled and
   chopped
60 g (2¼ oz) **butter**, cut into cubes
3 tablespoons **verjuice** or **white wine**

125 ml (4 floz/½ cup) **cream
   (whipping)**
4 x 200 g (7 oz) **eye fillet steaks**
2 tablespoons **red wine**
2 tablespoons **green peppercorns in
   brine**, drained
4 tablespoons **veal glaze**
1 tablespoon finely chopped **parsley**

Preheat the oven to 190°C (375°F/Gas 5). Place the tomatoes on a roasting tray covered with baking paper, drizzle with half the olive oil and season with salt and pepper. Bake for 12–15 minutes, or until just softening. Cut each truss in half.

Put the potatoes and celeriac in a saucepan of water. Bring to the boil, reduce the heat to medium and simmer for 12–15 minutes, or until soft. Drain and return to the pan over medium heat with half of the butter. Fry for 1 minute, or until just colouring. Add the verjuice and reduce by half. Remove from the heat, stir in the cream and mash or purée until smooth. Season with salt and pepper.

Brush the steaks with the remaining olive oil and season. Heat a heavy-based frying pan over high heat. Sear the steaks for 2 minutes on each side. Place on a baking tray and cook in the oven for a further 3–5 minutes for medium–rare, or until cooked to your liking. Cover with foil and set aside to rest.

Reduce the heat to medium and add the wine and peppercorns. Deglaze the pan for 30 seconds to 1 minute. Stir in the veal glaze and cook for a further 1–2 minutes, or until warmed through. Whisk in the remaining butter, remove from the heat and stir in the parsley. Serve the steaks on a bed of mash topped with the sauce and served with roasted tomatoes.

singapore black pepper crab

serves 4–6

3 tablespoons **kecap manis**

3 tablespoons **oyster sauce**

3 teaspoons **caster (superfine) sugar**

2 kg (4 lb 8 oz) **raw blue swimmer crabs**

1½ tablespoons **peanut oil**

40 g (1½ oz) **butter**

1½ tablespoons finely chopped fresh **ginger**

6 large **garlic cloves**, finely chopped

1–2 small **red chillies**, deseeded and finely chopped

1½ tablespoons freshly cracked **black pepper**

1½ teaspoons **ground white pepper**

¼ teaspoon **ground coriander**

2 **spring onions (scallions)**, finely sliced

1 handful **coriander (cilantro) leaves**, roughly chopped

Put the kecap manis, oyster sauce, sugar and 3 tablespoons of water in a small bowl and stir to combine, then set aside.

Pull back the apron on each crab and remove the top shell. Discard the intestines and pull off the grey feathery gills. Cut each crab into four pieces. Crack the legs with crab crackers or a meat mallet to allow the flavours to permeate the meat.

Heat the peanut oil in a large wok over high heat. Stir-fry the crab pieces in batches for about 5 minutes, or until the shell is bright orange and flesh is almost cooked, then remove from the wok.

Add the butter, ginger, garlic, chilli, black and white pepper and ground coriander to the wok and stir-fry for 30 seconds, or until fragrant. Add the sauce mixture and stir to combine. Bring to the boil and cook for 2 minutes, or until glossy. Return the crab to the wok and toss to coat in the sauce. Cook for 2–3 minutes further to finish cooking the crab meat then garnish with the spring onion and coriander leaves and serve immediately.

tip 1.5 kg (3 lb 5 oz) prawns (shrimp) in the shell can be substituted for the crab.

sichuan-peppered duck with honey sauce

serves 4

2 tablespoons **sichuan pepper**, dry-fried until fragrant

1 teaspoon **five-spice powder**

1 1/2 teaspoons **salt**

120 g (4 1/4 oz/1 cup) **cornflour (cornstarch)**

1 **Chinese barbecued duck**, removed from bone, cut into 2 cm (3/4 inch) cubes

270 ml (9 1/2 fl oz) **vegetable oil**

300 g (10 1/2 oz/1 bunch) **choy sum**, chopped into 5 cm (2 inch) pieces

2 teaspoons **sesame oil**

4 cm (1 1/2 inch) piece fresh **ginger**, finely diced

185 ml (6 fl oz/3/4 cup) **chicken stock**

1 1/2 tablespoons **honey**

steamed jasmine rice, to serve

Crush the pepper, five spice and salt to a fine powder using a mortar and pestle. Combine with the cornflour in a large bowl.

Toss the barbecued duck through the flour. Meanwhile, heat 250 ml (9 fl oz/1 cup) of the vegetable oil in a frying pan.

When hot, add the duck to the oil in batches. When crisp and golden, remove the duck and drain on paper towel.

Put a wok on medium–high heat, add the remaining vegetable oil and the sesame oil. Add the ginger and fry until softened. Add the choy sum and stir-fry for 1 minute.

Add the chicken stock and simmer for 2 minutes, or until the choy sum is tender. Remove the choy sum and reduce the cooking liquid by half. Add the honey and put the duck and choy sum back in the liquid. Toss to coat, and serve with steamed jasmine rice.

fragrant poached chicken with sichuan seasoning

serves 4

250 ml (9 fl oz/1 cup) **light soy sauce**

250 ml (9 fl oz/1 cup) **Chinese rice wine**

150 g (5 1/2 oz/heaped 2/3 cup) **sugar**

1 large piece (5 cm/2 inches) fresh **ginger**, unpeeled, sliced

3 **garlic cloves**, roughly chopped

1/2 teaspoon **ground star anise**

2 **cinnamon sticks**

1 strip **orange zest**, pith removed

1/2 teaspoon **five-spice powder**

1/2 teaspoon **sesame oil**

1 1/2 teaspoons **sichuan pepper**

1.5 kg (3 lb 5 oz) **whole chicken**, wing tips removed

1 teaspoon **vegetable oil**

1 tablespoon **salt**

lemon wedges and **steamed bok choy**, to serve

In a large saucepan, combine the soy, rice wine, sugar, ginger, garlic, star anise, cinnamon, orange zest, five spice, sesame oil, and 1/2 teaspoon of the sichuan pepper. Bring to the boil, add 400 ml (14 fl oz) of water and reduce to a simmer for 15 minutes.

Wash the chicken and submerge into the above stock, breast side down. Bring back to the boil and simmer for 30 minutes covered, turning the chicken over for the last 10 minutes. Turn off the heat and let the chicken cool in the stock. Drain the chicken on a wire rack. Preheat the oven to 220°C (425°F/Gas 7).

Put the remaining sichuan pepper into an ovenproof dish and place in the oven for 5 minutes, or until fragrant.

Put the chicken on a roasting tray and brush with vegetable oil. Place in the oven for 20–25 minutes, or until crisp and golden. Crush the sichuan pepper with 1 tablespoon of salt into a fine powder. Slice the lemon into eight wedges.

Chop the chicken into pieces and serve with the lemon, sichuan pepper mixture and steamed bok choy.

pork, snow pea and sichuan pepper stir-fry

serves 4

2 teaspoons **sichuan pepper**

1 tablespoon **sesame oil**

1 tablespoon **vegetable oil**

2 **garlic cloves**, crushed

3 cm (1 1/4 inch) piece fresh **ginger**, grated

300 g (10 1/2 oz) **pork fillet**, cut into thin strips

200 g (7 oz) **button mushrooms**, sliced

3 tablespoons **oyster sauce**

2 teaspoons **chilli bean paste**

1 teaspoon **Chinese black vinegar (chinkiang)**

150 g (5 1/2 oz) **snow peas (mangetout)**, trimmed

steamed jasmine rice, to serve

Heat the oven to 200°C (400°F/Gas 6). Put the sichuan pepper into a small ovenproof dish and roast for 5 minutes, or until fragrant. Cool and crush to a fine powder with a mortar and pestle.

Put the sesame and vegetable oils into a wok and heat until almost smoking. Add the garlic, ginger and sichuan pepper and stir-fry for 30 seconds.

Add the pork and stir-fry for about 3 minutes, or until no longer pink. Add the sliced mushrooms, oyster sauce, chilli bean paste, black vinegar, and 3 tablespoons of water and simmer for 2 minutes.

Toss through the snow peas and simmer for 2 more minutes. Serve immediately with steamed jasmine rice.

tip Chilli bean paste and Chinese black vinegar (chinkiang) are available from Asian supermarkets.

spiced spatchcocks with wild rice stuffing

serves 4

stuffing

105 g (3¹/2 oz/¹/2 cup) combined **wild** and **white rice**

¹/2 teaspoon **salt**

40 g (1¹/2 oz) **butter**

1 stem **lemon grass**, white part only

¹/2 teaspoon **lemon zest**

1 tablespoon finely chopped **coriander (cilantro) leaves**

1 tablespoon **soy sauce**

marinade

1 teaspoon **sichuan pepper**, crushed

1 teaspoon **coriander seeds**, crushed

1 teaspoon **sea salt flakes**

1 **red bird's eye chilli**, split in half, deseeded and finely chopped

1 tablespoon chopped **coriander (cilantro) leaves**

1 tablespoon grated fresh **ginger**

2 **garlic cloves**, crushed

2 tablespoons **soy sauce**

1 teaspoon **sesame oil**

4 x 500 g (1 lb 2 oz) **spatchcocks (poussin)**

olive oil, for roasting

roasted pumpkin (winter squash) and **steamed bok choy (pak choy)**, to serve

Spoon the **stuffing** mixture into the **spatchcock** cavities.

Brush all over with the **marinade**.

To make the stuffing, in a small saucepan bring 185 ml (6 fl oz/3/4 cup) of water, the rice and salt to the boil stirring occasionally. Lower the heat, cover and simmer very gently for 10 minutes. Remove from the heat and allow to stand for 5 minutes. Stir in the butter, lemon grass, zest, coriander and soy sauce while still warm. Set aside to cool.

Put the marinade ingredients into a small food processor and process until smooth. When the stuffing is cool, stuff the cavities of each of the spatchcocks. Brush the outside of each with the marinade, cover and refrigerate for 2 hours.

Preheat the oven to 190°C (375°F/Gas 5). Place the spatchcocks onto large roasting trays. Lightly coat with oil and roast, basting regularly, for 50 minutes to 1 hour, or until golden and juices run clear when pierced with a sharp knife. Serve the spatchcocks with roasted pumpkin and steamed bok choy.

tip Spatchcocks can be cut in half down the backbone after cooking using a pair of kitchen shears. This can make presentation and eating easier.

peppery prawn noodle salad

serves 4

dressing

1 teaspoon **sichuan pepper**

2 **spring onions (scallions)**, finely
chopped

1 tablespoon grated fresh **ginger**

1 tablespoon **soy sauce**

1 tablespoon **fish sauce**

1/4 teaspoon **sesame oil**

1 tablespoon **lime juice**

1 teaspoon **soft brown sugar**

100 g (31/2 oz) **mung bean vermicelli**

700 g (1 lb 9 oz) **cooked king prawns
(shrimp)**, peeled and deveined,
tails intact

1/2 **telegraph (long) cucumber**, sliced
in half, seeds removed and sliced
on diagonal

2 large **vine-ripened tomatoes**, sliced
into wedges

140 g (5 oz/12/3 cups) **bean sprouts**,
trimmed

1 large handful **mint**

1 handful **coriander (cilantro) leaves**

3 **spring onions (scallions)**, sliced

20 g (3/4 oz/1/4 cup) **crisp fried shallots**

In a small bowl, combine the dressing ingredients. Soften the vermicelli according
to packet instructions and cut with a pair of scissors.

Toss the prawns, cucumber, tomatoes, bean sprouts, mint, coriander, spring onions
and noodles together with the dressing. Divide among four plates, top with the
fried shallots and serve immediately.

tip Crisp fried shallots are available from Asian supermarkets, or from the
Asian section in some large supermarkets.

wasabi popcorn

makes 1 large bowl

4 tablespoons **peanut oil**

115 g (4 oz/1/2 cup) **popcorn kernels (popping corn)**

1 teaspoon **salt**

40 g (11/2 oz) **butter**, melted

3 teaspoons **wasabi paste**

2 teaspoons **caster (superfine) sugar**

Heat the oil in a large saucepan over medium–high heat. Drop a couple of pieces of popcorn kernels into the oil and if they spin, the oil is hot enough to cook the popcorn. Add the kernels and salt and place the lid on the pan.

When you start to hear the corn pop, shake the pan occasionally until the popping increases then slows down dramatically. Remove from the heat but keep the lid on until the popping stops completely. Meanwhile, melt the butter in a small saucepan, and stir in the wasabi and sugar. Tip the popcorn into a large bowl and drizzle over half the butter mixture, toss, then add the remaining butter mixture. Season to taste with more salt, if necessary, and serve warm.

sashimi salad with wasabi dressing

serves 4–6

600 g (1 lb 5 oz) **sashimi-grade tuna** or **salmon**

1/2 small **daikon**

4 handfuls **mizuna** or **baby rocket (arugula) leaves**

1 **Lebanese (short) cucumber**

wasabi dressing

2 teaspoons **wasabi paste**

1 **garlic clove**, crushed

1/2 teaspoon finely grated fresh **ginger**

1/4 teaspoon **caster (superfine) sugar**

1 tablespoon **lime juice**

1 tablespoon **mirin**

1 1/2 tablespoons **rice vinegar**

2 tablespoons **vegetable oil**

1/4 teaspoon **toasted sesame oil**

soy sauce, to season

Cut the fish into very thin, even slices with a sharp knife. Overlap the fish slices, circling inwards, to form a thin cover over a large serving plate. Cover and refrigerate until ready to use.

Peel the daikon, then using the fine tooth blade on a Japanese mandolin, or a very sharp knife and a steady hand, finely julienne the daikon then squeeze out any excess moisture. Chop the mizuna into 3 cm (1 1/4 inch) lengths. If using baby rocket, keep whole. Very finely slice the cucumber lengthways to form long thin ribbons (a vegetable peeler is good for this). Refrigerate all the salad ingredients until chilled.

To make the dressing, whisk together the wasabi, garlic, ginger, sugar, lime juice, mirin, rice vinegar, vegetable and sesame oils. Season to taste with a few drops of soy sauce and a small pinch of salt and set aside.

When ready to serve, combine the daikon, mizuna and cucumber, then toss together with the dressing. Place the salad mixture in the centre of the plate, drizzle any excess dressing over the fish and serve immediately.

vegetable tempura with wasabi soy

serves 4

wasabi soy

4 tablespoons **salt-reduced soy sauce**

2 teaspoons **wasabi paste**

tempura batter

150 g (5¹/2 oz/1¹/4 cups) **plain (all-purpose) flour**

60 g (2¹/4 oz/¹/2 cup) **cornflour (cornstarch)**

2 **eggs**

vegetable oil, for deep-frying

200 g (7 oz) **orange sweet potato**, cut into 1 cm (¹/2 inch) thick slices

200 g (7 oz) **carrots**, cut into thick sticks

175 g (6 oz/1 bunch) **asparagus**, trimmed, cut into 4–5 cm (1¹/2–2 inch) pieces

100 g (3¹/2 oz) **green beans** or **snow peas (mangetout)**, trimmed

1 **red capsicum (pepper)**, cut into large chunks

To make the wasabi soy, put the soy sauce and wasabi in a small bowl. Mix until well combined, then set aside.

To make the tempura batter, Put the flour, cornflour and a pinch of salt in a large bowl. Mix well to combine. Whisk 250 ml (9 fl oz/1 cup) iced water and the eggs together. Add to the flour mixture and mix until just combined. Do not overmix, it doesn't matter if there are lumps in the batter.

Preheat the oven to 200°C (400°F/Gas 6). Line a large baking tray with paper towel. Heat the oil in a large wide-based saucepan over medium–high heat until it reaches 180°C (350°F), or until a cube of bread dropped in the oil browns in 15 seconds. Dip the sweet potato into the batter, carefully shaking off any excess. Add to the oil and cook for 3–4 minutes, or until the batter is crisp and light golden. Use a slotted spoon to transfer to the paper towel. Once drained, transfer to the baking tray. Place in the oven to keep warm and crisp while repeating with the carrots, asparagus, beans and capsicum.

Serve the vegetable tempura immediately with wasabi soy.

roast chicken with wasabi chive butter

serves 4

60 g (2¼ oz) **butter**, softened

2 tablespoons **wasabi paste**

1 **garlic clove**, crushed

20 g (¾ oz/1 bunch) **chives**, snipped

2 kg (4 lb 8 oz) **whole chicken**, rinsed well and patted dry

1 teaspoon **vegetable oil**

¼ teaspoon **sesame oil**

¼ **lemon**

steamed Asian greens and **chives**, to serve

Preheat the oven to 200°C (400°F/Gas 6). Put the butter, wasabi, garlic and chives in a small bowl and combine well. Starting at the opening of the chicken, carefully use your fingers to loosen the skin over the whole breast of the chicken. Place the butter under the skin of the chicken and smooth over to evenly distribute.

Combine the vegetable and sesame oils and smear over the entire chicken. Tie the legs together with string. Squeeze the lemon quarter over the chicken, then sprinkle liberally with sea salt flakes. Place on a rack in a roasting pan and cook for 1 hour 15 minutes, or until the juices run clear when the thickest part of the thigh is pierced with a skewer.

Rest for 10 minutes before carving. Drizzle the pan juices over the meat. Serve with steamed Asian greens, garnish with chives, and sprinkle with a little more sea salt.

prawn and wasabi mayonnaise rolls

makes 6

600 g (1 lb 5 oz) **cooked prawns (shrimp)**, peeled and deveined

4 tablespoons **whole-egg mayonnaise**

3 teaspoons **lemon juice**

11/4 teaspoons **wasabi paste**

2 teaspoons finely chopped **mint**, plus extra whole leaves for topping

6 **mini bread rolls**

butter, for spreading (optional)

1 **Lebanese (short) cucumber**, finely sliced

Roughly chop the prawns, then combine with the mayonnaise, lemon juice, wasabi and mint. Season to taste.

Cut through the bread rolls, leaving them hinged. Pull a little bread out from the inside of the top half of the roll to form a slight hollow.

Spread each roll with a little butter, if desired, then lay a few slices of cucumber over the bottom half of each roll. Top with a couple of mint leaves, then fill the rolls with the prawn mixture and serve.

sweet

sugar and spice

A hit of the sweet stuff can be just the ticket at the end of a meal — or to complement a hot afternoon brew. Owing to their sweet nature, this collection of spices are very popular. Found in everything from perfume to ice cream, chewing gum to shampoo — the sweet spices not only taste sensational in food and drink products, but they also add a sweetened, mellow aroma. Of all the spices across the world, it is the sweet ones that have retained much of the sense of luxury that they held in earlier times. This seems especially true of spices such as cinnamon, vanilla and cardamom — just a sprinkle or dash still adds a touch of festivity to a dish. If used in moderation, these spices won't overwhelm a dish but will enhance the flavours of the ingredients and add a subtle, mellow and utterly enticing taste. Can a dessert or baked treat be truly delightful without a sweet spice? Your tastebuds can only tell you no.

Of the many varieties, green **cardamom** from South India and Sri Lanka is superior. Use the pod or the seeds whole or ground. The seeds have a sweet, mild flavour.

Cinnamon is used to flavour many sweet Western and savoury Eastern dishes. The inner bark of this Sri Lankan native is dried and sold as quills or sticks.

243

The knobbly rhizome of a tropical plant, **ginger** is a Southeast Asian native. This spice is available in many forms and has a sharp, sweet taste with a warming effect.

Nutmeg is the hard kernel of an evergreen plant. The best flavour — warm, sweet and spicy — is from the whole nutmeg, freshly grated just prior to use.

A Chinese native, **star anise** is a star-shaped fruit containing seeds, and has a strong, licorice-like flavour. This spice is used extensively in Arabic and Asian cuisine.

Vanilla comes from the bean of a climbing orchid vine native to Central America. The best-quality beans have a warmly sweet, caramel vanilla aroma and flavour.

245

cardamom coffee ice cream

serves 4

6 **green cardamom pods**

375 ml (13 fl oz/1½ cups) **milk**

250 ml (9 fl oz/1 cup) **thick (double/heavy) cream**

1 tablespoon **instant coffee granules**

115 g (4 oz/½ cup) **caster (superfine) sugar**

5 **egg yolks**

Lightly crush the cardamom pods and put in a saucepan with the milk, cream and coffee granules. Heat gently until the mixture just reaches boiling point, remove from the heat and leave to infuse for 20 minutes.

In a bowl, beat the sugar and egg yolks together until pale and light, stir in the infused cream mixture and strain into a clean saucepan. Heat gently, stirring constantly over low heat for 8–10 minutes, or until the mixture thickens to coat the back of the spoon. Do not allow the custard to boil or it will curdle.

Remove from the heat and leave to cool completely. Pour into a shallow container, cover and freeze until frozen around the edges. Put into a cold bowl and beat with electric beaters until thick. Return to the shallow container and refreeze. Repeat this process 2–3 times until the ice cream is a thick consistency. Pour into a container and freeze.

If using an ice cream machine, chill the mixture for 1 hour and then churn in an ice cream maker until frozen. Serve at once or freeze in a plastic container until required.

honey and cardamom biscuits

makes 24

200 g (7 oz) **unsalted butter**

150 g (5¹/2 oz/²/3 cup) **caster (superfine) sugar**

3 tablespoons **honey**

250 g (9 oz/2 cups) **plain (all-purpose) flour**

1 teaspoon **baking powder**

80 g (2³/4 oz/³/4 cup) **ground almonds**

2 teaspoons **ground cardamom**

icing (confectioners') sugar, for dusting

Preheat the oven to 170°C (325°F/Gas 3). In a small saucepan, melt the butter, sugar and honey over medium heat, stirring until the sugar dissolves.

In a large bowl, sift the flour and baking powder. Stir in the ground almonds and cardamom. Make a well in the centre and add the butter mixture. Stir until just combined.

Place tablespoons of the mixture onto baking trays lined with baking paper. Flatten slightly with the base of a glass and bake for 15–18 minutes, or until lightly golden. Rest on trays for 5 minutes before transferring to a wire rack to cool completely. Dust lightly with icing sugar.

raspberry and cardamom cake with honey syrup

serves 6–8

125 g (4¹/2 oz) **unsalted butter**, softened, cut into cubes

125 g (4¹/2 oz/¹/2 cup) **caster (superfine) sugar**

2 **eggs**

1 teaspoon **vanilla extract**

250 g (9 oz/2 cups) **self-raising flour**

2 teaspoons **ground cardamom**

125 ml (4 fl oz/¹/2 cup) **milk**

150 g (5¹/2 oz) **raspberries**, fresh or frozen

whipped cream, to serve

honey syrup

175 g (6 oz/¹/2 cup) **honey**

2 tablespoons **caster (superfine) sugar**

¹/4 teaspoon **vanilla extract**

Preheat the oven to 180°C (350°F/Gas 4). Grease a 20 cm (8 inch) round cake tin and line the base with baking paper.

Using an electric mixer, beat the butter until soft. Add the caster sugar gradually and beat until the mixture is pale and creamy. Add the eggs and vanilla, and beat until the mixture is well combined.

Sift the flour and cardamom together. Using a large metal spoon, fold the flour into the creamed mixture alternately with the milk, starting with the flour and ending with flour. Do not overmix.

Lightly fold the raspberries into the mixture. Pour the batter into the prepared tin and gently smooth the surface. Bake for 40–45 minutes, or until a skewer inserted into the centre comes out clean. Remove the cake from the oven and insert a thin metal skewer all over the cake.

To make the honey syrup, put 125 ml (4 fl oz/1/2 cup) of water, and the honey and sugar in a small saucepan and stir over low heat until the sugar has dissolved. Remove the pan from the heat and add the vanilla extract. Pour half of the honey syrup over the cake. Allow the cake to stand for 10 minutes. Turn the cake out. Serve warm with whipped cream and the remaining honey syrup.

Using a large metal **spoon**, fold the **raspberries** into the mixture.

Pour half of the **honey** syrup over the **cake** and stand for 10 minutes.

253

pumpkin, coconut and cardamom steamed puddings

makes 6 individual puddings

125 g (41/2 oz) **unsalted butter**, softened

115 g (4 oz/1/2 cup) **caster (superfine) sugar**

3 **eggs**

90 g (31/4 oz/3/4 cup) **plain (all-purpose) flour**

11/2 teaspoons **ground cardamom**

1 teaspoon **baking powder**

125 g (41/2 oz/1 cup) grated **pumpkin (winter squash)**

40 g (11/2 oz/2/3 cup) **shredded coconut**

ice cream, to serve

Preheat the oven to 180°C (350°F/Gas 4). Using electric beaters, cream the butter and sugar until light and fluffy. Add the eggs one at a time, beating well after each addition. Gently fold through the sifted flour, cardamom and baking powder. Stir through the pumpkin and coconut.

Grease 6 x 185 ml (6 fl oz/3/4 cup) pudding or dariole moulds with melted butter. Divide the pudding mixture between the prepared moulds. Place the puddings in a large baking tin and pour in enough hot water to come halfway up the sides of the moulds. Cover the baking tin with a sheet of baking paper then foil. Pleat the foil down the centre and fold tightly around the edges of the pan to seal.

Bake the puddings for 30–35 minutes, or until the puddings spring back when lightly touched. Remove the puddings from the water bath, stand for 5 minutes, then turn the puddings onto serving plates. Serve hot with ice cream.

cardamom and yoghurt bavarois

makes 8

4 **egg yolks**

115 g (4 oz/1/2 cup) **caster (superfine) sugar**

200 g (7 oz) **vanilla yoghurt**

185 ml (6 fl oz/3/4 cup) **milk**

1 teaspoon **ground cardamom**

1/2 teaspoon **vanilla extract**

1 tablespoon **gelatine powder**

300 ml (101/2 fl oz) **cream (whipping)**, lightly whipped

Beat the egg yolks and sugar until thick and pale. Combine the yoghurt, milk, cardamom and vanilla in a saucepan and stir over low heat until just coming to the simmer. Pour the warm milk mixture over the yolks and whisk to combine. Return to a clean saucepan and stir over medium heat for 7–8 minutes, or until the custard has thickened enough to coat the back of a wooden spoon. Remove from the heat.

Dissolve the gelatine in 3 tablespoons of hot water and stir it through the custard.

Set the custard aside to cool completely, then gently fold through the cream.

Divide the mixture between 8 x 125 ml (4 fl oz/1/2 cup) moulds and refrigerate for 2–3 hours to set. To unmould and serve, dip a blunt knife into warm water and run the tip around the edge of the mould. Dip the mould into a bowl of warm water for a few seconds, shaking slightly to loosen. Place the serving plate over the mould, invert and remove the mould.

cinnamon chocolate shortbread

makes 32

200 g (7 oz/1²/3 cups) **plain (all-purpose) flour**

40 g (1¹/2 oz/¹/3 cup) **unsweetened cocoa powder**

1¹/2 teaspoons **ground cinnamon**

250 g (9 oz) **unsalted butter**

60 g (2¹/4 oz/¹/2 cup) **icing (confectioners') sugar**

caster (superfine) sugar, for sprinkling

Preheat the oven to 160°C (315°F/Gas 2–3). Line two baking trays with baking paper. Sift together the flour, cocoa and cinnamon. Using electric beaters, beat the butter and icing sugar until light and creamy. Using a large metal spoon, fold in the sifted flour mixture. Turn the dough out onto a lightly floured surface and knead gently until smooth.

Roll out the dough between two sheets of baking paper until 1 cm (¹/2 inch) thick. Using a 7 cm (2³/4 inch) star cutter, cut out the biscuits. Place on the prepared trays, leaving room for spreading. Prick the dough with a fork, sprinkle the top with the caster sugar and refrigerate for 30 minutes.

Bake for 15–18 minutes, swapping trays halfway through cooking. Allow to cool on the trays.

cinnamon semi freddo

serves 8–10

230 g (8¹/2 oz/1 cup) **caster (superfine) sugar**

4 **eggs**, at room temperature, separated

600 ml (21 fl oz) **thickened (whipping) cream**

1¹/2 teaspoons **ground cinnamon**

pinch **salt**

tinned **baby apples**, to serve (optional)

Line a 21 x 11 x 7 cm (8¹/4 x 4¹/4 x 2³/4 inch) loaf (bar) tin with a double layer of plastic wrap, allowing the excess to overhang onto the sides. Using electric beaters, beat the sugar and egg yolks in a bowl until thick and pale. In a separate bowl, whisk the cream to soft peaks, then gently fold through the egg yolk mixture along with the cinnamon.

In a separate bowl, whisk the egg whites with the salt until firm peaks form. Gently fold through the mixture. Pour into the prepared tin and cover with a double layer of plastic wrap. Place in the freezer overnight, or until firm.

Transfer the semi freddo from the freezer to the refrigerator 5 minutes before serving. Turn out onto a board, remove the plastic wrap and cut into slices. Serve with baby apples, if desired.

white chocolate and cinnamon mousse with fresh blueberries

serves 4

2 **eggs**, separated

4 tablespoons **milk**

1 teaspoon **ground cinnamon**

180 g (6¹/2 oz) **white chocolate**, chopped

2 teaspoons **gelatine powder**

185 ml (6 fl oz/3/4 cup) **thickened (whipping) cream**

150 g (5¹/2 oz/1 cup) fresh **blueberries**, plus extra to serve

Put the egg yolks, milk and cinnamon in a small heavy-based saucepan and whisk together. Add the chopped chocolate and stir over low heat until the mixture is smooth.

Put 2 tablespoons of hot water in a small bowl, and sprinkle the gelatine over the surface. Stand for a few minutes to soften, then whisk with a fork to dissolve. Stir into the warm chocolate mixture. Set over a bowl of cold water to cool.

Using electric beaters, beat the egg whites until soft peaks form. In a separate bowl, beat the cream until soft peaks form. Fold the cream into the chocolate mixture, then fold in the egg whites.

Divide the blueberries between serving glasses or bowls. Spoon the chocolate mixture into the serving dishes. Cover and refrigerate for several hours, or until set. Top with extra blueberries and serve.

tip Use fresh blueberries, as frozen blueberries will discolour the mousse.

cinnamon pecan biscotti

makes 30 biscuits

2 **eggs**, at room temperature

250 g (9 oz/heaped 1 cup) **caster (superfine) sugar**

280 g (10 oz/2¼ cups) **plain (all-purpose) flour**

¹/2 teaspoon **baking powder**

2 teaspoons **ground cinnamon**

125 g (4¹/2 oz/1¹/4 cups) **pecans**

Preheat the oven to 170°C (325°F/Gas 3). Line a baking tray with baking paper. Using electric beaters, beat the eggs and sugar for 2 minutes, or until pale and thick. Add the sifted flour, baking powder, cinnamon and pecans. Use a flat-bladed knife to mix to a soft dough. Turn out onto a lightly-floured surface and knead until the mixture comes together.

Divide the mixture into two equal portions. Shape each portion into logs about 25 cm (10 inches) long and 8 cm (3¼ inches) wide. Place the logs onto the prepared tray, leaving room for spreading, and bake for 35–40 minutes, or until lightly coloured. Set aside to cool completely.

Using a serrated knife, cut the logs into 1 cm (¹/2 inch) thick slices and place in a single layer, cut side down, on the tray. Bake for 15–20 minutes, or until crisp and lightly golden in colour, turning halfway through cooking. Allow to cool completely on the tray.

spiced cheesecake slice

makes 10 slices

250 g (9 oz) **wheatmeal biscuits (cookies), such as Granita**

1/2 teaspoon **ground cinnamon**, plus 1 teaspoon extra

1/2 teaspoon **ground nutmeg**

100 g (31/2 oz) **unsalted butter**, melted

500 g (1 lb 2 oz) **cream cheese**, at room temperature

4 tablespoons **honey**

3 **eggs**, at room temperature

85 g (3 oz/2/3 cup) **sultanas (golden raisins)**

1 teaspoon **ground cinnamon**, extra

Brush a 27 x 17 cm (103/4 x 61/2 inch) rectangular shallow tin with melted butter and line the base and two long sides with baking paper. Put the biscuits in a food processor with the cinnamon and nutmeg and process into crumbs. Add the butter and process until well combined. Press firmly into the prepared tin and refrigerate until firm. Preheat the oven to 170°C (325°F/Gas 3).

Using electric beaters, beat the cream cheese and honey together until the mixture is creamy. Add the eggs one at a time, beating well after each addition. Stir through the sultanas. Pour the mixture over the base. Sprinkle over the extra cinnamon, and swirl gently with a thick bamboo skewer to create a swirled effect on the top. Bake for 30–35 minutes, or until just set. Cool in the tin, then cut into pieces to serve.

caramelized pineapple and ginger tarte tatin

serves 6–8

165 g (5³/4 oz/1¹/3 cups) **plain (all-purpose) flour**

1¹/2 teaspoon **ground ginger**

85 g (3 oz) **unsalted butter**, cut into cubes

1 **egg yolk**

50 g (1³/4 oz) **glacé ginger**, chopped

100 g (3¹/2 oz) **unsalted butter**, extra

160 g (5³/4 oz/scant ³/4 cup) **caster (superfine) sugar**

1 **pineapple**, peeled, quartered lengthways, cored and cut into
   5 mm (1/4 inch) slices

thick (double/heavy) cream, to serve

Use the **pulse** button to process just until the **mixture** comes together.

Cook the **pineapple** until tender, and the **caramel** is reduced and thickened slightly.

Put the flour, ginger and butter in a food processor and process until the mixture resembles fine breadcrumbs. Add the egg yolk, glacé ginger and 2–3 tablespoons of water and pulse until the mixture comes together. Turn out onto a lightly floured surface and bring together in a ball. Cover with plastic wrap and place in the fridge for 20 minutes to rest.

Melt the extra butter in a 24 cm (9$1/2$ inch) ovenproof frying pan over low heat, add the sugar and stir until dissolved. Increase the heat to medium and cook, stirring, until the sugar starts to caramelize and turn golden brown (the mixture may go grainy then will go smooth). Reduce the heat to medium–low and add the pineapple slices. Cook for 15 minutes, or until the pineapple is tender and the caramel mixture is reduced and thickened slightly.

Preheat the oven to 180°C (350°F/Gas 4). Roll out the pastry between two sheets of baking paper to a disc slightly larger than the top of the frying pan. Lay the pastry over the top of the pineapple and tuck the edges down the side of the pan. Cook in the preheated oven for 35–40 minutes, or until the pastry is golden in colour.

Carefully turn the tart onto a large serving plate, cut into slices and serve with cream.

ginger and pistachio biscuits

makes 25 biscuits

100 g (3¹/2 oz) **unsalted butter**

125 g (4¹/2 oz/²/3 cup) **soft brown sugar**

1 teaspoon **vanilla extract**

2 **eggs**, at room temperature

250 g (9 oz/2 cups) **plain (all-purpose) flour**

1¹/2 teaspoons **baking powder**

2 teaspoons **ground ginger**

100 g (3¹/2 oz/²/3 cup) **pistachio nuts**, roughly chopped

white chocolate, for drizzling (optional)

Preheat the oven to 170°C (325°F/Gas 3). Line two baking trays with baking paper. Using electric beaters, beat together the butter, sugar and vanilla until light and creamy. Add the eggs, one at a time, and beat until well combined.

Fold through the combined sifted flour, baking powder and ginger. Stir through the pistachio nuts. Using lightly floured hands, roll tablespoons of the mixture into balls, place on the prepared trays, allowing room for spreading. Flatten the biscuits slightly with a lightly floured fork.

Bake for 15–18 minutes, or until crisp and golden, swapping the trays halfway through cooking. Allow to cool on the trays for 5 minutes before transferring to a wire rack to cool. Drizzle the biscuits with white chocolate, if desired

steamed ginger pudding

serves 8

60 g (2¼ oz/½ cup) **plain (all-purpose) flour**

185 g (6½ oz/1½ cups) **self-raising flour**

2 teaspoons **ground ginger**

1 teaspoon **mixed spice**

½ teaspoon **ground cinnamon**

125 g (4½ oz) **unsalted butter,** cut into cubes

125 ml (4 fl oz/½ cup) **golden** or **maple syrup**

3 tablespoons **treacle** or **molasses**

2 **eggs**, lightly whisked

75 g (2½ oz/⅓ cup) **glacé ginger,** chopped

custard, to serve

Lightly grease a 1.5 litre (52 fl oz/6 cup) capacity heatproof pudding basin with melted butter, and line the base with a round of baking paper. Brush a large sheet of foil with butter. Lay a sheet of baking paper on top, creating a pleat in the centre.

Sift the flours, ground ginger, mixed spice,. and cinnamon into a large bowl and make a well in the centre. Put the butter, golden syrup, and treacle into a saucepan, and stir over medium–low heat until the butter has melted and is well combined, then allow to cool slightly. Pour into the flour well, along with the eggs and chopped ginger. Stir until well combined, but do not over-beat as the pudding will become tough.

Pour the mixture into the prepared basin, cover with the foil and paper, paper side down. Tie securely with string under the lip of the basin. Place the basin on a trivet in a large deep saucepan. Carefully pour boiling water into the pan down the side of the basin to come halfway up the side of the basin, and bring to the boil over high heat. Reduce the heat to medium–low, cover with a lid and simmer for 2 hours, or until a skewer inserted into the centre comes out clean. Add more boiling water to the pan when necessary.

Remove the pudding from the pan. Allow to stand for 5 minutes before turning out onto a serving plate. Cut into slices and serve with custard.

ginger crunch slice

makes 16 slices

125 g (41/2 oz) **unsalted butter,**
  softened, chopped

115 g (4 oz/1/2 cup) **caster (superfine)**
  sugar

1 teaspoon **vanilla extract**

165 g (53/4 oz/11/3 cups) **plain**
  (all-purpose) flour

2 teaspoons **ground ginger**

1 teaspoon **baking powder**

ginger icing (frosting)

50 g (13/4 oz) **unsalted butter**

11/2 tablespoons **golden** or **dark**
  corn syrup

2 teaspoons **ground ginger**

90 g (31/4 oz/3/4 cup) **icing**
  (confectioners') sugar

3 tablespoons chopped **crystallized**
  ginger

Preheat the oven to 180°C (350°F/Gas 4). Line the base and two long sides of a 27 x 18 cm (103/4 x 7 inch) shallow tin with baking paper.

Put the chopped butter, sugar and vanilla in a bowl and beat with electric beaters until creamy. Sift together the combined plain flour, ginger and baking powder. Use a metal spoon to stir in the flour mixture in two batches until well incorporated.

Use your fingers to press firmly and evenly into the prepared tin. Bake for 20 minutes, or until pale golden and firm to touch.

Meanwhile, to make the ginger icing, put the butter, golden syrup, ginger, and icing sugar in a small saucepan. Stir over low heat until smooth. Pour and spread the icing evenly over the slice while the slice is hot. Mark into 16 slices and scatter over the crystallized ginger. Set aside to cool, then cut, using marks as a guide.

tip This slice will keep refrigerated in an airtight container for up to 8 days.

ginger fruit loaf

makes 1 loaf

375 g (13 oz) **mixed dried fruit**

160 g (5³/4 oz/1 cup) chopped **pitted dried dates**

75 g (2¹/2 oz/¹/3 cup) **glacé ginger**, chopped

60 g (2¹/4 oz) **unsalted butter**, chopped

185 g (6¹/2 oz/1 cup) **soft brown sugar**

1 tablespoon **golden** or **dark corn syrup**

1 teaspoon **vanilla extract**

2 **eggs**, lightly beaten

185 g (6¹/2 oz/1¹/2 cups) **plain (all-purpose) flour**

1 teaspoon **baking powder**

2 teaspoons **ground ginger**

1 teaspoon **ground nutmeg**

20 **blanched almonds**

Put the mixed fruit, dates, glacé ginger, butter, brown sugar, golden syrup, vanilla essence and 310 ml (10³/4 fl oz/1¹/4 cups) water in a saucepan. Bring slowly to the boil, then simmer over low heat for 5 minutes. Set aside to cool.

Preheat the oven to 160°C (315°F/Gas 2–3). Grease the base and sides of a 25 x 11 cm (10 x 4¹/4 inch) loaf (bar) tin and line the base with baking paper.

Stir the beaten eggs into the cooled fruit mixture. Sift together the flour, baking powder and spices. Stir the flour mixture into the fruit mixture and mix until smooth.

Spoon into the prepared tin and smooth the surface. Arrange the almonds over the surface. Bake for 1 hour 20 minutes, or until a skewer inserted in the centre comes out clean. Cover with foil if the surface and almonds are browning too much. Leave to cool in the tin for 10 minutes, then turn out onto a wire rack to cool. Serve cut into thick slices.

tip Store in an airtight container for up to 2 weeks. This loaf is also suitable to freeze.

spiced caramelized bananas

serves 4

50 g (1³/4 oz) **unsalted butter**

2 tablespoons **soft brown sugar**

¹/2 teaspoon **ground nutmeg**

¹/4 teaspoon **ground allspice**

4 **bananas**, peeled and sliced lengthways

grated **zest** and **juice** of 1 **orange**

1 tablespoon **rum**

2 tablespoons lightly roasted **pecans** or **walnuts**, chopped

freshly grated **nutmeg**, to sprinkle

ice cream, to serve

Put the butter, sugar, nutmeg and allspice in a frying pan over medium heat. Mix until combined and cook for 1 minute, or until the sugar has dissolved. Add the bananas, cut side down, and cook for 2 minutes, or until a little softened.

Remove the bananas to a serving plate. Add the orange zest and juice to the frying pan and stir for 2 minutes, or until mixture thickens and is syrupy. Stir in the rum. Spoon the sauce over the bananas. Sprinkle with the chopped nuts and sprinkle with some freshly grated nutmeg. Serve warm with ice cream.

peach and custard tart

serves 6

185 g (6¹/2 oz/1¹/2 cups) **plain (all-purpose) flour**

2 tablespoons **icing (confectioners') sugar**

90 g (3¹/4 oz) **unsalted butter**, chilled, cut into cubes

2 large **peaches**

2 **eggs**, lightly whisked

2 tablespoons **caster (superfine) sugar**

160 ml (5¹/4 fl oz) **thickened (whipping) cream**

³/4 teaspoon **ground nutmeg**

Put the flour, icing sugar and butter in a food processor and process until the mixture resembles fine breadcrumbs. Add 3–4 tablespoons of iced water and pulse until the mixture comes together and forms a dough. Turn out onto a lightly floured surface and bring together in a ball. Cover with plastic wrap and place in the fridge for 20 minutes to rest.

Preheat the oven to 190°C (375°F/Gas 5). Lightly grease a 24 cm (9¹/2 inch) loose-bottomed fluted flan tin with melted butter, then place on a baking tray. Roll out the pastry between two sheets of baking paper and line the prepared tin, trimming the edges. Line the pastry shell with a piece of crumbled baking paper, and pour in rice or beans to cover the base. Cook in the oven for 15 minutes, then remove the paper and rice and cook for a further 10 minutes, or until the pastry is cooked and lightly golden in colour. Allow the pastry to cool.

Reduce the oven temperature to 170°C (325°F/Gas 3). Cut the peaches in half and remove the seeds. Finely slice the peaches and arrange in a circular pattern over the pastry base. Whisk together the eggs, sugar, cream and nutmeg. Carefully pour the mixture over the peaches. Bake in the oven for 25–30 minutes, or until the mixture is just set. Allow to cool completely before serving.

hot brandy eggnog

serves 4

4 **egg yolks**

80 g (2¾ oz/⅓ cup) **caster (superfine) sugar**

500 ml (17 fl oz/2 cups) **milk**

¼ teaspoon **ground nutmeg**, plus extra for dusting

¼ teaspoon **vanilla extract**

3 tablespoons **brandy** (or more to taste)

125 ml (4 fl oz/½ cup) **cream (whipping)**, whipped

Whisk the egg yolks and sugar together in a bowl until pale and creamy. Bring the milk just to the boil, then slowly pour onto the egg mixture, stirring constantly.

Pour into a clean saucepan, and stir over very low heat for 10–15 minutes, without boiling, until thickened slightly.

Remove from the heat and stir in the nutmeg and vanilla, then the brandy. Serve warm topped with whipped cream and sprinkled with a little more nutmeg.

pear and almond cake

serves 12

almond pear topping

50 g (13/4 oz) **unsalted butter**, melted

2 tablespoons **soft brown sugar**

1 teaspoon **ground nutmeg**

425 g (15 oz) tin **pear halves**, drained and halved

75 g (21/2 oz/1/2 cup) finely chopped **blanched almonds**, lightly toasted

cake batter

125 g (41/2 oz) **unsalted butter**

115 g (4 oz/1/2 cup) **caster (superfine) sugar**

1 teaspoon **vanilla extract**

2 **eggs**

55 g (2 oz/1/2 cup) **ground almonds**

250 g (9 oz/2 cups) **self-raising flour**

1 teaspoon **ground nutmeg**

125 ml (4 fl oz/1/2 cup) **milk**

cream (whipping), to serve

Preheat the oven to 180°C (350°F/Gas 4). Lightly grease and line the base of a 23 cm (9 inch) tin with baking paper. In a bowl, combine the melted butter, brown sugar and nutmeg. Evenly pour over the base of the tin. Arrange the pear quarters over and scatter the almonds over the pear slices.

Put the butter, caster sugar and vanilla into a mixing bowl and beat with electric beaters for 2–3 minutes, or until creamy. Add the eggs, one at a time, beating well between each addition.

Stir in the ground almonds. Fold in the sifted flour and nutmeg in two to three batches, alternating with the milk. Carefully spoon the batter into the tin on top of the pears and smooth the surface.

Bake for 40 minutes, or until a skewer inserted in the centre comes out clean. Cool in the tin for 20 minutes, then remove and cool on a wire rack, pear side up. Carefully peel away the baking paper. Cut into wedges and serve warm with cream.

tip This cake will keep in an airtight container for up to 5 days. It is also suitable to freeze.

Arrange the **pears** over the base of the tin, and **scatter** with almonds.

Spoon the **batter** over the pears and **smooth** the surface.

289

nutmeg and saffron panna cotta

makes 6

500 ml (17 fl oz/2 cups) **cream (whipping)**

185 ml (6 fl oz/3/4 cup) **milk**

100 g (31/2 oz/scant 1/2 cup) **caster (superfine) sugar**

1 teaspoon **ground nutmeg**

pinch **saffron threads**

21/2 teaspoons **gelatine powder**

fresh fruit, to serve

Put the cream, milk, sugar, nutmeg and saffron in a saucepan. Heat over low heat until the mixture just comes to the boil. Remove from the heat immediately and cool until just warm.

Place 2 tablespoons of hot water in a small bowl, and sprinkle the gelatine over the surface. Stand for a few minutes to soften, then whisk with a fork to dissolve. Stir into the cream mixture and leave to cool.

When cool, strain the mixture and pour into 6 x 125 ml (4 fl oz/1/2 cup) dariole moulds. Refrigerate overnight to set. To unmould and serve, dip a blunt knife into warm water and run the tip around the edge of the mould. Dip the mould into a bowl of warm water for a few seconds, shaking slightly to loosen. Place the serving plate over the mould, invert and remove the mould. Repeat with the other moulds. Serve the panna cotta with fresh fruit.

spiced glazed oranges

serves 4

250 ml (9 fl oz/1 cup) **orange juice**, strained

2 tablespoons **caster (superfine) sugar**

4 **star anise**

2 **cinnamon sticks**, broken in half

4 **oranges**, peeled and cut into 1 cm (1/2 inch) slices

vanilla ice cream, to serve

Put the juice, sugar, star anise and cinnamon sticks in a deep-sided frying pan. Stir over low heat for 3 minutes, or until the sugar has dissolved. Bring to the boil, reduce the heat and simmer for 3 minutes, or until the liquid becomes syrupy.

Add the orange slices and simmer for a further 7 minutes, or until the oranges have softened slightly and are well coated with the syrup. Serve the oranges warm, drizzled with syrup and a scoop of vanilla ice cream.

strawberry and star anise sorbet

serves 4

115 g (4 oz/1/2 cup) **caster (superfine) sugar**

3 **star anise**

750 g (1 lb 10 oz) **strawberries**

3 tablespoons **lime juice**

Put 250 ml (9 fl oz/1 cup) of water, and the sugar and star anise in a small saucepan over low heat and stir until the sugar has dissolved. Increase the heat and boil for 1 minute. Set aside to cool completely. Discard the star anise.

Hull and purée the strawberries. Combine the purée, lime juice and cold sugar syrup in a bowl and stir to combine. Pour the mixture into an ice cream maker and churn according to the manufacturer's instructions until the sorbet is just firm. Spoon into a container and freeze until ready to serve.

chocolate star anise cake with coffee caramel cream

serves 8

200 g (7 oz) good-quality **dark chocolate**, roughly chopped

125 g (41/2 oz) **unsalted butter**

4 **eggs**

2 **egg yolks**

115 g (4 oz/1/2 cup) **caster (superfine) sugar**

50 g (13/4 oz) **plain (all-purpose) flour**, sifted

2 teaspoons **ground star anise**

50 g (13/4 oz) **ground almonds**

coffee caramel cream

125 ml (4 floz/1/2 cup) **thick (double/heavy) cream**

3 tablespoons **soft brown sugar**

2 tablespoons brewed **espresso coffee**, cooled

Preheat the oven to 190°C (375°F/Gas 5). Grease and line a 23 cm (9 inch) springform cake tin.

Put the chocolate and butter in a bowl set over a saucepan of gently simmering water, but do not allow the base of the bowl to come into contact with the water. Heat gently until the mixture is melted.

Put the eggs, egg yolks and sugar into a bowl and beat with a electric beaters for 5 minutes until thickened. Fold in the flour, ground star anise and ground almonds and then fold in the melted chocolate mixture until evenly combined (the mixture should be runny at this stage).

Pour the mixture into the prepared tin and bake for 30–35 minutes, or until a skewer inserted in the middle comes out clean. Cool in the tin for 5 minutes and then remove and cool on a wire rack.

To make the coffee caramel cream, whip the cream, sugar and coffee together until soft peaks form and the colour is a soft caramel. Serve the cold cake cut into wedges with a spoonful of the coffee caramel cream.

plum and star anise jam

makes 4 cups

1 kg (2 lb 1 oz) firm **plums**, quartered

1 kg (2 lb 4 oz) **caster (superfine) sugar**

125 ml (4 fl oz/1/2 cup) **lemon juice**

3 **star anise**

1 teaspoon **ground ginger**

In a heavy-based saucepan, put the plums, sugar, lemon juice, 125 ml (4 fl oz/ 1/2 cup) of water, star anise, and ground ginger.

Bring the ingredients in the saucepan to a boil, stirring until the sugar has dissolved. Reduce the heat to medium and simmer for 35–40 minutes, stirring occasionally.

Place a saucer in the freezer to chill. Test the setting consistency of the jam by placing a spoonful onto the chilled saucer. Cool slightly and run your finger through the jam, if it crinkles it is ready.

Remove any froth from the surface of the jam and remove the whole star anise with a metal spoon. Pour the jam into prepared hot sterilized jars and seal.

pear and raspberry crumble

serves 4

6 large **pears** (1.5 kg/3 lb 5 oz), ripe but firm

2 tablespoons **caster (superfine) sugar**

3 **star anise**

125 g (4 1/2 oz/1 cup) **raspberries**

125 g (4 1/2 oz/1 cup) **plain (all-purpose) flour**

95 g (3 1/4 oz/1/2 cup) **soft brown sugar**

100 g (3 1/2 oz) **unsalted butter**, cut into cubes

ice cream, to serve

Preheat the oven to 190°C (375°F/Gas 5). Peel, quarter and core the pears, then cut each piece in half lengthways. Put into a large saucepan, and sprinkle the sugar over. Add 1 tablespoon of water and the star anise. Cover and bring to the boil.

Cook, covered, over medium–low heat for 10 minutes, stirring occasionally, until the fruit is tender but still holds its shape. Drain the pears and discard the star anise, and transfer to a 1.5 litre (52 fl oz/6 cup) capacity ovenproof dish. Sprinkle the raspberries over the pears.

Combine the flour, sugar and butter in a bowl. Use your fingertips to rub the butter into the flour until the mixture resembles coarse breadcrumbs. Sprinkle over the fruit, then bake for 20–25 minutes, until golden brown. Stand for 5 minutes, then serve with ice cream.

vanilla coconut cupcakes

makes 12

150 g (5¹/2 oz) **unsalted butter**, cut
   into cubes
115 g (4 oz/¹/2 cup) **caster (superfine)
   sugar**
2 teaspoons **vanilla extract**
2 **eggs**
185 g (6¹/2 oz/1¹/2 cups) **plain
   (all-purpose) flour**
1 teaspoon **baking powder**
45 g (1¹/2 oz/¹/2 cup) **desiccated
   coconut**
125 ml (4 fl oz/¹/2 cup) **milk**

vanilla icing (frosting)

60 g (2¹/4 oz/1 cup) **flaked coconut**
20 g (³/4 oz) **unsalted butter**, cut
   into cubes
2 teaspoons **vanilla extract**
185 g (6¹/2 oz/1¹/2 cups) **icing
   (confectioners') sugar**, sifted

Preheat the oven to 180°C (350°F/Gas 4). Line 12 x 125 ml (4 fl oz/¹/2 cup) muffin holes with paper cases.

Put the butter, sugar and vanilla extract in a bowl and beat with electric beaters for 2–3 minutes, or until thick and creamy. Add the eggs, one at a time, and beat in each until well combined.

Sift together the flour and baking powder. Use a metal spoon to stir the sifted flour and baking powder in two lots. Stir in the desiccated coconut and the milk.

Put spoonfuls evenly into the paper cases. Bake for 18–20 minutes, or until firm and golden brown. Cool on a wire rack.

For the vanilla glacé icing, spread the flaked coconut on a tray and lightly toast for 2–3 minutes in the oven. Put the butter in a small bowl and pour over 2 teaspoons of hot water to soften the butter. Add the vanilla essence. Put the icing sugar in a bowl, add the butter mixture and mix together until smooth, adding a little more water if necessary to make a spreading consistency.

Use a small spatula to spread the cooled cakes with the icing and dip each into the coconut flakes. Set aside to firm the icing.

vanilla bean and honeycomb ice cream

makes 1 litre (35 fl oz/4 cups)

375 ml (13 fl oz/1¹/2 cups) **milk**

1 **vanilla bean**, split lengthways

170 g (6 oz/3/4 cup) **caster (superfine) sugar**

4 **egg yolks**

500 ml (17 fl oz/2 cups) **cream (whipping)**

100 g (3¹/2 oz/1 cup) chopped **honeycomb**

Put the milk and vanilla bean in a saucepan and heat to just below boiling point. Put the sugar and egg yolks in a bowl and whisk for 2–3 minutes until thick and creamy.

Gradually pour the hot milk into the egg mixture, whisking constantly until smooth. Return the mixture to the saucepan and stir until the mixture coats the back of a metal spoon. Take care not to boil. This should take 1–2 minutes depending on the heat of the milk.

Strain into a clean bowl. Scrape the vanilla seeds from the bean with a knife and whisk into the custard. Cool and stir over a bowl of ice or refrigerate until cold. Stir in the cream.

Pour into a shallow container, cover and freeze until frozen around the edges. Put into a cold bowl and beat with electric beaters until thick. Return to the shallow container and refreeze. Repeat this process 2–3 times until the ice cream is a thick consistency. Fold through the honeycomb. Pour into a container and freeze.

If using an ice cream machine, refrigerate the custard for several hours, stir in the honeycomb then churn according to the manufacturer's instructions. Pour into a container and freeze.

tip This ice cream can be stored in an airtight container in the freezer for up to 2 weeks.

roasted spiced pears and strawberries

serves 4

170 g (6 oz/3/4 cup) **caster (superfine) sugar**

2 **vanilla beans**, split lengthways

2 **star anise**

1 **cinnamon stick**, broken in half

4 firm **pears**, peeled and cut into quarters

250 g (9 oz/12/3 cups) **strawberries**, hulled, cut in half if large

Greek-style yoghurt, to serve

Preheat the oven to 170°C (325°F/Gas 3). Put 310 ml (103/4 fl oz/11/4 cups) of water, and the sugar, vanilla beans, star anise and cinnamon in an ovenproof dish. Place in the oven and cook for 10 minutes, stirring once, until the sugar dissolves.

Add the pears to the syrup. Cover with foil and cook for 35–45 minutes, or until almost tender, turning once in the syrup. Add the strawberries and turn to coat in the syrup. Cover with foil and cook for a further 5 minutes, or until the strawberries soften.

Set aside to cool to room temperature and serve with yoghurt.

berry and vanilla brûlée tart

serves 6–8

sweet shortcrust pastry

250 g (9 oz/2 cups) **plain (all-purpose) flour**

125 g (41/2 oz) **unsalted butter**, cut into cubes

2 tablespoons **caster (superfine) sugar**

berry custard filling

2 **egg yolks**

250 ml (9 fl oz/1 cup) **cream (whipping)**

125 ml (4 fl oz/1/2 cup) **milk**

1 **vanilla bean**, split lengthways

55 g (2 oz/1/4 cup) **caster (superfine) sugar**

60 g (21/4 oz/1/2 cup) fresh **raspberries**

80 g (23/4 oz/1/2 cup) fresh **blueberries**

55 g (2 oz/1/4 cup) **caster (superfine) sugar**, for sprinkling

Line the pastry **shell** with a sheet of baking paper and fill with **rice** and/or baking weights.

Scatter the **berries** over the **pastry** base.

To make the sweet shortcrust pastry, put the flour and butter in a food processor. Process in short spurts until the mixture resembles fine breadcrumbs. Briefly pulse in the sugar. With the motor running, add 2 tablespoons of iced water, adding a little more water, if necessary, until the dough comes roughly together. Turn out and press into a ball. Wrap in plastic wrap and refrigerate for at least 30 minutes.

Preheat the oven to 200°C (400°F/Gas 6). Heat a baking tray. Roll the pastry between two sheets of baking paper. Fit into a 23 cm (9 inch) flan tin with removable base. Line the pastry with a sheet of baking paper and weigh down with rice and/or baking beads. Bake for 15 minutes on the preheated hot tray until lightly golden. Remove the paper and rice and/or baking beads and cook for a further 10 minutes. Reduce the oven temperature to 170°C (325°F/Gas 3). Cool the pastry case.

To make the brûlée filling, lightly beat together the egg yolks and cream in a bowl. Put the milk, vanilla bean and sugar in a saucepan and stir over low heat until the sugar has dissolved. Increase the heat and bring to the boil. Remove the vanilla bean and scrape the seeds with a knife. Whisk into the hot milk, together with the combined eggs and cream.

Scatter the berries over the base of the pastry. Carefully pour the custard over the berries. Place on a hot baking tray and bake for 35–40 minutes, or until the custard has set. Cool then refrigerate to firm.

Preheat the grill (broiler). Sprinkle the pie evenly with the sugar. Place under the hot grill for 7–8 minutes, or until the sugar has melted and caramelized. Cool and cut into wedges to serve.

tips This tart is unsuitable to freeze. Fresh berries are better as frozen berries bleed into the custard.

311

vanilla scented rhubarb ice

serves 8

650 g (1 lb 7 oz) **rhubarb** (about 6 stems)

230 g (81/2 oz/1 cup) **caster (superfine) sugar**

1 **vanilla bean**

cream (whipping), to serve (optional)

Wash the rhubarb and trim the ends. Chop the stems into 2 cm (3/4 inch) lengths, and put into a saucepan. Add the sugar and 250 ml (9 fl oz/1 cup) water, and stir over a low heat until the sugar has dissolved.

Split the vanilla bean in half lengthways, and scrape out the seeds. Add the seeds and bean to the pan.

Bring to the boil and cook over a medium–low heat, partially covered, for 5 minutes, until the rhubarb is very soft. Cool slightly, remove the vanilla bean, then purée in a food processor until smooth.

Pour into a 1.25 litre (44 fl oz/5 cup) capacity plastic container, cover tightly and freeze for 4 hours. Use a fork to break up the crystals, and freeze again for another 4 hours.

To serve, break up the crystals again with a fork, then spoon into small serving glasses. Drizzle a little cream over, and serve immediately.

blends

mix it up

One spice hero per dish might seem plenty, thank you very much, but put a few complementary spices together and you have a potential celebration in your mouth. Why have just one when you can have two or more? Of course a spice blend should have a developed, rounded flavour — the spices should complement and not compete with each other — and the blend should enhance the ingredients in a dish. Many spice blends have been available since the earliest days of spice trading. Indeed many countries and regions across the world have favourite blends, initially developed by using native spices, that go best alongside national dishes. The blends in this chapter are classics of the spice world — tried and tested over many years and used in many dishes. Of course you should feel free to alter the ratio of the ingredients, to enhance a favoured flavour, but remember that balance is the key to all blends.

mortar and pestle

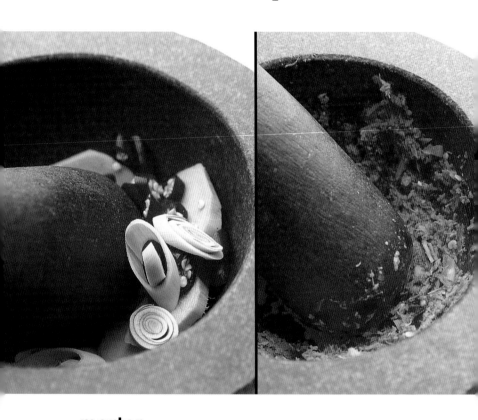

The **mortar** is a heavy bowl, and the **pestle** a heavy blunt implement, usually made of stone such as granite, or of ceramic.

Ingredients are pounded to make a **paste** or powder.

electric grinder

Electric **spice** grinders are available from kitchenware stores, or you could use an **electric** coffee grinder, kept specifically for the task.

A small **food** processor may do the trick, depending on the **quantity** of spice to be ground.

chermoula

makes 4 tablespoons

2 **garlic cloves**, crushed

1 large handful **parsley**

1 large handful **coriander (cilantro) leaves**

2 teaspoons **cumin seeds**, toasted and ground

2 teaspoons **Hungarian hot paprika**

1/2 teaspoon **ground turmeric**

1 tablespoon **lemon juice**

2 tablespoons **extra virgin olive oil**

Put all the ingredients, except the oil, in a blender. Season with salt and pepper. Blend until finely chopped. With the motor running, drizzle in the oil and blend to a paste. You can also use a mortar and pestle.

Store in an airtight container in the fridge. Use within 2 days.

A **Moroccan** spice blend which also contains fresh **herbs** and is a 'wet' mixture. Can be used as a marinade or sauce.

sardines with chermoula stuffing

serves 4

105 g (3¹/2 oz/1¹/3 cups) **fresh breadcrumbs** (see tip)

1/4 **preserved lemon**, pith removed, washed and finely chopped

6 **green olives**, pitted and finely chopped

1/2 **red chilli**, deseeded and finely chopped

1¹/2 tablespoons **chermoula paste**

16 **sardine fillets**

olive oil, for drizzling

lemon wedges, to serve

Preheat the oven to 200°C (400°F/Gas 6). Lightly grease a large ovenproof dish. Set aside 25 g (1 oz/1/3 cup) of the breadcrumbs. In a bowl, combine the remaining breadcrumbs, the preserved lemon, olives, chilli and chermoula paste and mix well.

Lay eight of the sardine fillets, in a single layer, skin side down, in the dish. Divide a generous layer of the chermoula stuffing over the sardines. Lay the remaining eight sardines, skin side up, on top. Lightly scatter each with the reserved breadcrumbs and drizzle with olive oil.

Cover the dish with foil. Bake for 15 minutes. Remove the foil and bake for a further 10 minutes, or until cooked and golden. Serve immediately with lemon wedges.

tip Use 4 slices white bread, crusts removed, to make 105 g (3¹/2 oz/ 1¹/3 cups) crumbs.

marinated chicken wings with yoghurt tomato dip

serves 4

12 **chicken wings**

marinade

2 tablespoons **vegetable oil**

2 tablespoons **honey**

2 tablespoons **chermoula paste**

1 tablespoon **lemon juice**

yoghurt tomato dip

250 g (9 oz/1 cup) **Greek-style yoghurt**

1 **tomato**, deseeded and finely chopped

1/4 **red onion**, finely chopped

2 teaspoons **chermoula paste**

Remove the tips from the chicken wings and cut the wings in half through the joint.

Combine all the marinade ingredients in a large non-metallic dish. Add the chicken wings and toss well to coat evenly. Cover and marinate for several hours, or overnight.

Preheat the oven to 180°C (350°F/Gas 4). Line a large baking tray with foil. Drain the wings, reserving the marinade. Put the wings on a rack on the baking tray. Bake for 50–60 minutes, or until cooked and golden brown. Brush with the reserved marinade two to three times during cooking.

To make the yoghurt dip, combine all the ingredients in a bowl. Serve the warm chicken wings with the yoghurt dip.

madras curry powder

makes 2/3 cup

3 tablespoons **coriander seeds**

1 1/2 tablespoons **cumin seeds**

1 tablespoon **black mustard seeds**

1 teaspoon **black peppercorns**

1 tablespoon **ground turmeric**

2 teaspoons **garlic powder**

1/2 teaspoon **chilli powder**

1/2 teaspoon **ground ginger**

In a large frying pan, dry-fry the coriander seeds, cumin seeds, mustard seeds and black peppercorns for 1 minute, or until aromatic. Put in a food processor together with the remaining spices. Process until smooth.

Store in an airtight container for up to 1 month.

This **versatile** mixture is flavoursome rather than hot. It can be used with **fish**, chicken, lamb, beef or vegetables.

sweet potato soup

serves 4

1 tablespoon **vegetable oil**

1 large **onion**, chopped

4 **garlic cloves**, crushed

2 teaspoons grated fresh **ginger**

1 tablespoon **madras curry powder**

1 kg (2 lb 4 oz) **orange sweet potato**, peeled and chopped into
   5 cm (2 inch) chunks

1 litre (35 fl oz/4 cups) **vegetable** or **chicken stock**

400 g (14 oz) **coconut milk**

1 small handful **coriander (cilantro) leaves**, chopped

fried Asian shallots and **naan bread** or **chappati**, to serve

Heat the oil in a large saucepan. Add the onion and cook over medium heat for 3 minutes, or until softened. Add the garlic, ginger and curry powder. Stir for a further 1 minute. Add the sweet potato and stir to coat in the mixture.

Pour over the stock. Bring to the boil then lower the heat. Cover and simmer for 20 minutes, or until the sweet potato is cooked.

Cool slightly, then process in batches, using a food processor, until smooth. Return to the saucepan and stir in the coconut milk and coriander, reserving some coriander for garnish. Stir and reheat for 2–3 minutes. Serve in bowls topped with a sprinkle of fried Asian shallots and the remaining coriander. Serve with heated naan bread or chappati.

tips This soup has a mild flavour but if you prefer a stronger curry flavour add an extra 2 teaspoons curry powder. Fried onion flakes are available from Asian food stores.

madras-style beef curry

serves 6

1 1/2 tablespoons **madras curry powder**

270 ml (9 1/2 fl oz) **coconut milk**

4 tablespoons **vegetable oil**

2 large **onions**, finely chopped

3 **garlic cloves**, crushed

1.25 kg (2 lb 12 oz) **chuck** or **gravy beef**, trimmed and cut into
    3 cm (1 1/4 inch) cubes

250 ml (9 fl oz/1 cup) **beef stock**

2 **tomatoes**, peeled and chopped

1 teaspoon **lemon juice**

cooked basmati rice, to serve

1 handful **coriander (cilantro) leaves**, to serve

Mix the curry powder with a little of the coconut milk to form a paste. Heat the oil in a large heavy-based 3 litre (104 fl oz/12 cup) capacity flameproof casserole dish on the stovetop.

Fry the onion, stirring frequently, for 5 minutes, or until lightly golden. Stir in the garlic and curry paste and cook for a further 2 minutes, or until aromatic.

Add the meat and stir to coat in the spice mixture. Add the stock and tomatoes. Bring to the boil, then reduce the heat to a low simmer. Cover and cook for 2 hours, stirring occasionally.

Stir in the remaining coconut milk and lemon juice. Serve with rice and garnish with coriander leaves.

tip To peel the tomatoes, plunge in a bowl of boiling water for 30 seconds, then drain, cool and peel.

five-spice powder

makes 3 1/2 tablespoons

1 1/2 tablespoons **ground star anise**

3 teaspoons **ground fennel**

3 teaspoons **ground cassia**

1 teaspoon **ground sichuan pepper**

1/2 teaspoon **ground cloves**

Put all the ground spices in a small bowl and combine well.

Store in an airtight container for up to 1 month.

A traditional **Chinese** mixture made from five **ground** spices, with a dominant star anise flavour.

five-spice chicken stir-fry with celery

serves 4

3 tablespoons **cornflour (cornstarch)**

3 teaspoons **five-spice powder**, plus
1/2 teaspoon extra

125 ml (4 fl oz/1/2 cup) **chicken stock**

2 tablespoons **light soy sauce**

1 tablespoon **Chinese rice wine** or
sherry

2 teaspoons **rice vinegar**

2 teaspoons **caster (superfine) sugar**

1/2 teaspoon **sesame oil**

500 g (1 lb 2 oz) boneless, skinless
chicken breasts, trimmed and cut
into thin strips

3 tablespoons **vegetable oil**, for frying

4 **spring onions (scallions)**, white part
chopped, green part reserved

2 sticks **celery**, cut into 3 cm (1 1/4 inch)
slices diagonally

1 **long red chilli**, deseeded and finely
chopped

2 **garlic cloves**, finely chopped

2 teaspoons grated fresh **ginger**

steamed jasmine rice, to serve

Combine the cornflour and five-spice powder on a plate. Take 1 teaspoon of the mixture and put in a small bowl with a little stock to form a paste, then add the remaining stock, soy sauce, rice wine, rice vinegar, caster sugar, sesame oil and extra five-spice powder and set aside.

Pat the chicken breast strips dry with paper towel and toss in the combined flour and five-spice powder. Shake off any excess. Heat a wok until very hot and add 1 tablespoon of the oil. Stir-fry half the chicken for 3 minutes, or until cooked. Remove to a side plate, add another 1 tablespoon of oil and cook the remaining chicken. Remove to a side plate.

Heat the remaining tablespoon of oil. Stir-fry the white spring onions, celery, chilli, garlic and ginger for 2–3 minutes, or until aromatic.

Return the chicken and combined sauce to the wok. Stir-fry for 2 minutes, or until the sauce has thickened a little and the chicken is hot. Shred the reserved spring onions and use to garnish. Serve immediately with jasmine rice.

five-spice pork ribs

serves 4

1 kg (2 lb 4 oz) American-style **pork ribs**
shredded **spring onions (scallions)** (optional), to serve

marinade

125 ml (4 fl oz/1/2 cup) **tomato sauce (ketchup)**

2 tablespoons **Chinese rice wine** or **dry sherry**

2 tablespoons **light soy sauce**

2 tablespoons **honey**

1 tablespoon **sweet chilli sauce**

2 teaspoons **five-spice powder**

2 **garlic cloves**, crushed

Cut the pork ribs into individual ribs. Combine all the marinade ingredients in a large non-metallic bowl. Add the ribs and toss well to coat evenly. Cover and marinate for several hours, or overnight.

Preheat the oven to 180°C (350°F/Gas 4). Line a large baking tray with foil. Remove excess marinade from the ribs, reserving the remaining marinade. Put the ribs on a rack on the baking tray. Bake for 30 minutes, or until cooked and golden brown. Brush with the reserved marinade 1–2 times during cooking. Serve hot, garnished with spring onions if desired.

panch phora

makes 5 tablespoons

1 tablespoon **brown mustard seeds**

1 tablespoon **nigella seeds**

1 tablespoon **cumin seeds**

1 tablespoon **fennel seeds**

1 tablespoon **fenugreek seeds**

Put all the spices in a small bowl and combine well.

Store in an airtight container for up to 1 year.

A mixture of **whole** spices, used in Indian cookery. It is added to hot oil at the beginning of cooking, to **flavour** the oil.

339

eggplant coconut curry

serves 6

500 g (1 lb 2 oz) **slim eggplants (aubergines)**, trimmed and cut into
   3 cm (1¼ inch) chunks

4 tablespoons **vegetable oil**

1 tablespoon **panch phora**

2 teaspoons **ground cumin**

1 teaspoon **ground turmeric**

1 **red onion**, finely sliced

3 **garlic cloves**, chopped

1 **long green chilli**, deseeded and finely chopped

8 dried **curry leaves**

400 ml (14 fl oz) **coconut milk**

Put the eggplant in a colander and sprinkle with salt. Set aside for 15 minutes to sweat. Rinse, drain and pat dry with paper towel.

Heat 2 tablespoons of the oil in a large heavy-based non-stick frying pan. Fry the eggplant for 5 minutes, stirring frequently, or until lightly browned. Remove to a side plate.

Heat the remaining oil in the frying pan. Add the panch phora, cumin and turmeric and cook for 1 minute, or until aromatic. Add the onion and cook for 3 minutes, or until the onion is cooked.

Stir in the garlic, chilli and curry leaves and add the eggplant. Stir to coat in the spices. Stir in the coconut milk and 250 ml (9 fl oz/1 cup) of water. Season with salt.

Cook, stirring frequently, for 20 minutes, or until the eggplant is cooked and the sauce is thick. Serve hot or at room temperature.

tip Dried curry leaves are available from Asian food stores and some large supermarkets.

spicy fried potatoes

serves 4

600 g (1 lb 5 oz) **all-purpose potatoes**, peeled and cut into 3 cm (11/4 inch) cubes

3 tablespoons **vegetable oil**

1 tablespoon **panch phora**

2 teaspoons **ground cumin**

1/2 teaspoon **ground turmeric**

1/2 teaspoon **chilli powder**

1 **onion**, finely sliced

2 **garlic cloves**, finely chopped

1 tablespoon **lime juice**

2 tablespoons chopped **coriander (cilantro) leaves**, to serve

Put the potato cubes in a saucepan of boiling water. Bring back to the boil and cook for 5 minutes. Drain, refresh under cold running water and drain again. Pat dry with paper towel.

Heat the oil in a large non-stick frying pan. Add the panch phora and remaining spices and cook for 1 minute, or until aromatic. Stir in the onion and cook for 5 minutes on medium heat, or until the onion is cooked.

Add the garlic and potato cubes and stir to coat in the spices. Season with salt. Stir often and fry the potato for 15 minutes, or until the potato is cooked and golden brown. To serve, sprinkle with lime juice and the coriander leaves.

ras el hanout

makes 2 tablespoons

2 teaspoons **coriander seeds**

11/2 teaspoons **cumin seeds**

1/2 teaspoon **cardamom seeds**

1/2 teaspoon **fennel seeds**

1/2 teaspoon **black peppercorns**

1 teaspoon **ground turmeric**

1 teaspoon **ground cinnamon**

1/2 teaspoon **hot paprika**

1/4 teaspoon **salt**

Put the seeds and peppercorns in a frying pan. Dry-fry for 1 minute, or until aromatic. Put in a food processor or mortar and pestle together with the remaining spices. Process until smooth.

Store in an airtight container for up to 1 month.

A Moroccan **spice** blend
whose name translates
roughly as 'top of the
shop', meaning it is the
best **quality**.

chargrilled vegetables and haloumi

serves 4

4 **thin or baby eggplant (aubergine)**, halved lengthways and cut into 3 cm (1¼ inch) pieces

2 **zucchini (courgettes)**, halved lengthwise, cut into 3 cm (1¼ inch) pieces

1 **red capsicum (pepper)**, cut into 4 cm (1½ inch) pieces

1 **yellow capsicum (pepper)**, cut into 4 cm (1½ inch) pieces

50 g (1¾ oz) fresh **baby corn**, halved lengthways

1 small **red onion**, cut into 4 wedges

4 tablespoons **olive oil**

1½ tablespoons **ras el hanout**, plus 2 teaspoons extra

2 **garlic cloves**, crushed

olive oil, for greasing

250 g (9 oz) **haloumi**, cut into 4 x 1 cm (½ inch) thick slices

1 handful **flat-leaf (Italian) parsley**, chopped

Put all the vegetables in a large bowl. Combine the oil with the ras el hanout and garlic. Pour over the vegetables and toss well. Set aside for at least 1 hour to marinate.

Heat a chargrill pan or barbecue grill plate and grease with oil. Cook the vegetables for 20 minutes, in batches if necessary, until tender and lightly charred. Remove to a side plate. Wipe down the chargrill or hotplate with paper towel.

Sprinkle one side of the haloumi slices with the extra ras el hanout. Coat the chargrill or grill plate with more oil. Fry the spiced side only for 1–2 minutes, or until golden. Arrange the haloumi slices, cooked side up, on serving plates. Pile the vegetables on top and scatter with parsley.

moroccan-style chicken with couscous salad

serves 4

couscous salad

500 ml (17 fl oz/2 cups) **apple juice**

370 g (13 oz/2 cups) **couscous**

1/2 small **red onion**, halved and finely
sliced lengthways

50 g (13/4 oz/1/3 cup) **pistachio nuts**,
toasted

8 **dried apricots**, chopped

60 g (21/4 oz/1/3 cup) **green olives**,
pitted and chopped

1/4 **preserved lemon**, pulp removed,
rinsed and finely chopped

1 small handful **mint**, roughly chopped

1 small handful **parsley**, roughly
chopped

2 tablespoons **plain (all-purpose) flour**

1 tablespoon **ras el hanout**

12 **chicken tenderloins**, trimmed

2–3 tablespoons **olive oil**

yoghurt dressing

250 g (9 oz/1 cup) **plain yoghurt**

2 tablespoons chopped **mint**

2 teaspoons **ras el hanout**

1 teaspoon **honey**

Heat the apple juice in a saucepan until hot but not boiling. Put the couscous in a bowl, pour over the apple juice, cover and set aside for 5 minutes. Fluff up with a fork. Toss the remaining salad ingredients through the couscous.

Meanwhile, combine the flour and ras el hanout on a flat plate. Coat the chicken tenderloins in the mixture and shake off the excess. Heat the oil in a large non-stick frying pan. Cook the chicken for 2–3 minutes on each side, or until cooked and golden. Add a little more oil as needed. Slice the chicken.

To make the yoghurt dressing, combine the ingredients in a bowl. To serve, pile the couscous onto serving plates, top with the chicken slices and spoon over the yoghurt dressing.

shichimi togarashi

makes 2 tablespoons

2 teaspoons **sancho** or **sichuan peppercorns**

1 teaspoon **white sesame seeds**

1 teaspoon **black sesame seeds**

2 teaspoons crushed **dried tangerine peel**

1 teaspoon finely chopped **nori**

1 teaspoon **chilli powder**

1 teaspoon **poppy seeds**

Grind the sancho or sichuan pepper and sesame seeds with a mortar and pestle or spice grinder. Combine with the remaining ingredients.

Store in an airtight container for up to 1 month.

A spice blend from **Japan**, which can be used in cooking, or at the **table** to be added as Westerners would use salt and pepper.

udon noodle and mushroom soup

serves 4

1.5 litres (52 fl oz/6 cups) **vegetable stock**

2 tablespoons **mirin**

2 teaspoons grated fresh **ginger**

1 teaspoon **wakame (dried seaweed) flakes**

150 g (5½ oz) fresh **shiitake mushrooms**, sliced

440 g (15½ oz) packet fresh **udon noodles**

2 **spring onions (scallions)**, sliced diagonally

75 g (2½ oz) **snow peas (mangetout)**, trimmed and finely sliced lengthways

50 g (1¾ oz) **bean sprouts**, trimmed

2 tablespoons **light soy sauce**

1 **nori sheet**, shredded

1 tablespoon **shichimi togarashi**, for sprinkling

Put the stock in a large saucepan and bring to the boil. Reduce the heat to a simmer. Add the mirin, ginger, wakame and sliced mushrooms. Simmer for 5 minutes.

Put the noodles in a large bowl and pour over boiling water. Leave for 1 minute to heat through. Drain, refresh under cold running water and separate the noodles, then set aside.

Add the spring onions, snow peas, bean sprouts, soy sauce and shredded nori to the stock and simmer for a further 2 minutes.

Divide the noodles among four large serving bowls. Ladle over the hot broth and vegetables. Sprinkle with the shichimi togarashi.

tip Wakame flakes and nori are available from some supermarkets and Asian food stores.

vegetable salad with shichimi togarashi

serves 4

2 **carrots**, peeled and cut into matchsticks

2 sticks **celery**, cut into matchsticks

200 g (7 oz) **snow peas (mangetout)**, trimmed and cut into fine slices lengthways

1 small **red capsicum (pepper)**, seeded and finely sliced

2 **spring onions (scallions)**, cut diagonally into fine slices

150 g (5 1/2 oz) **bean sprouts**, trimmed

6 **radishes**, finely sliced

1 tablespoon **shichimi togarashi**, for sprinkling

dressing

1 tablespoon **rice vinegar**

1 tablespoon **mirin**

1 tablespoon **vegetable oil**

2 teaspoons **fish sauce**

1 teaspoon **honey**

Bring a saucepan of water to the boil. Add the carrots, celery, snow peas and capsicum. Bring back to the boil. Cook for 1 minute, then drain and refresh under cold running water and drain again.

Put the blanched vegetables in a large bowl. Add the spring onions, bean sprouts, and radishes. Combine the dressing ingredients, pour over the vegetables and toss well.

Pile the salad onto a serving platter and sprinkle with the shichimi togarashi.

za'atar

makes 4 tablespoons

2 tablespoons **sesame seeds**

1 tablespoon **dried thyme**

2 teaspoons **sumac**

1/4 teaspoon **salt**

Grind the seeds and thyme in a grinder or with a mortar and pestle to a coarse texture. Stir in the sumac and salt.

Store in an airtight container for up to 1 month.

A **Middle Eastern**

mixture, unusual in that it

contains a spice, a herb and a

seed. Delicious sprinkled

on warmed Turkish bread.

broad bean, feta and preserved lemon salad

serves 4

350 g (12 oz/2¼ cups) **frozen broad (fava) beans**

1 **red capsicum (pepper)**, finely sliced

100 g (3½ oz) **firm feta cheese**, cut into cubes

1 tablespoon **za'atar**

¼ small **red onion**, finely sliced

125 g (4½ oz) **yellow baby tomatoes**, cut in half

¼ **preserved lemon**, pulp removed, washed and finely sliced

100 g (3½ oz) **mixed salad leaves**

orange dressing

2 teaspoons grated **orange zest**

2 tablespoons **orange juice**

2 tablespoons **olive oil**

1 teaspoon **honey**

1 teaspoon **za'atar**

Bring a saucepan of water to the boil. Add the broad beans and bring back to the boil. Cook for 5 minutes, drain, refresh under cold running water and peel the outer skins from the beans.

Meanwhile, in another small saucepan, blanch the red capsicum in boiling water for 1 minute, then drain, refresh and drain again. Sprinkle the feta cubes with the za'atar to coat on all sides. Combine all the dressing ingredients.

Put the broad beans, capsicum, onion and tomatoes in a large bowl. Add the preserved lemon. Pour over the dressing and toss. Add the feta cubes and toss gently. Put the salad leaves on serving plates and pile the combined mixture on top.

lamb and hummus wraps

serves 4

500 g (1 lb 2 oz) **minced (ground) lamb**

1 **onion**, finely chopped

2–3 **garlic cloves**, chopped

1 tablespoon **za'atar**, plus extra, for sprinkling

30 g (1 oz/1 cup) **coriander (cilantro) leaves**

olive oil

4 **Lebanese (large pitta) breads**, to serve

75 g (2¹/2 oz) **mixed salad leaves**

hummus

300 g (10¹/2 oz) tinned **chickpeas**

2 **garlic cloves**, crushed

1 tablespoon **tahini paste**

3 tablespoons **lemon juice**

Put the lamb, onion, garlic, za'atar and coriander leaves in a food processor and blend until smooth and pasty. Put into a bowl, cover and refrigerate for 1 hour.

With wet hands, form the meat into eight 12 cm (4¹/2 inch) elongated sausage shapes. Heat a barbecue flat plate or grill plate and coat with the oil. Coat the lamb with oil. Cook and turn for 8 minutes, or until evenly browned and cooked through.

Meanwhile, to make the hummus, drain the chickpeas, reserving the liquid and put in a food processor or blender. Add the garlic and tahini. With the motor running, add the lemon juice and 3 tablespoons of the reserved chickpea liquid. Process until smooth. Add a little more lemon juice and reserved liquid, if desired, and season with salt and black pepper.

Lightly brush one side of the Lebanese breads with oil and sprinkle with the za'atar. Put the unoiled side on the chargrill or hotplate for 2–3 minutes, or until heated through.

To serve, place the Lebanese breads on serving plates. Generously spread over the hummus. Top each with two of the lamb sausages and some salad leaves and roll up firmly.

baharat

makes 2 tablespoons

2 teaspoons **black peppercorns**

2 teaspoons **coriander seeds**

2 teaspoons **cumin seeds**

2 teaspoons **cloves**

seeds from 6 **green cardamom pods**

1/2 **cinnamon stick**, broken into small pieces

1 teaspoon **Hungarian paprika**

1 teaspoon **ground nutmeg**

Dry-fry the all the spices except the paprika and nutmeg in a small frying pan over medium heat, or until aromatic. Cool, then put in a food processor or spice mill with the paprika and nutmeg. Blend until finely ground.

Store in an airtight container for up to 1 month.

The name **baharat** means pepper. There are different variations, but they always contain **pepper** and allspice.

barbecue fish with green bean salad

serves 4

marinade

3 tablespoons **grapeseed oil**

2 teaspoons grated **lemon zest**

2 tablespoons **lemon juice**

2 teaspoons **baharat**

green bean salad

225 g (8 oz) **green beans**, trimmed

1 **zucchini (courgette)**

1 small **carrot**, peeled

1/2 **red onion**, finely sliced into wedges

salad dressing

2 tablespoons **grapeseed oil**

1 tablespoon **lemon juice**

1 teaspoon **honey**

1/2 teaspoon **baharat**

4 firm **white fish fillets** (800 g/
   1 lb 12 oz), such as **snapper**

olive oil

100 g (31/2 oz) **mixed salad leaves** or
   baby rocket (arugula) leaves

lemon wedges, to serve

To make the marinade, combine the oil, lemon zest and juice and the baharat in a non-metallic dish. Coat the fish in the marinade and set aside for 30 minutes.

To make the salad, shred or finely slice the beans. Using a vegetable peeler, cut the zucchini and carrot into fine strips. Put all the ingredients into a large bowl. Combine the salad dressing ingredients and just prior to serving, pour over the salad and toss well.

Preheat a barbecue flat plate or grill plate. Lightly coat with the oil. Cook the fillets for 1 minute on each side to seal, then lower the heat and cook for 2–3 minutes on each side, or until just cooked through. The cooking time will depend on the thickness of the fillets. Brush with the marinade one or two times.

To serve, divide the salad leaves or rocket onto serving plates, pile the bean salad over and top each with a fish fillet. Serve with lemon wedges.

veal casserole with gremolata

serves 4

3 tablespoons **olive oil**

1 large **onion**, chopped

1 stick **celery**, chopped

2 teaspoons **baharat**, plus
   1 tablespoon extra

3 **garlic cloves**, chopped

1 tablespoon **plain (all-purpose) flour**

4 large 5 cm (2 inch) thick pieces **veal
   osso buco**

30 g (1 oz) **butter**

125 ml (4 fl oz/1/2 cup) **dry white wine**

400 g (14 oz) tin **chopped tomatoes**

250 ml (9 fl oz/1 cup) **chicken** or **beef
   stock**

pasta, such as **risoni**, to serve

gremolata

1 handful finely chopped **parsley**

2 **garlic cloves**, finely chopped

finely grated zest of 1 **lemon**

Preheat the oven to 160°C (315°F/Gas 2–3). Heat 1 1/2 tablespoons of the oil in a heavy-based casserole dish. Cook the onion, celery and baharat for 3 minutes. Add the garlic and cook for a further 2 minutes, or until softened. Remove to a side dish.

Combine the flour and the extra baharat. Coat the cut sides of the meat in the flour mixture. Heat the remaining oil and the butter. Brown the veal on both sides over high heat. Arrange the veal in a single layer in the casserole dish. Add the white wine, bring to the boil and evaporate the wine by half.

Mix together the onion mixture and tomatoes and pour over the veal. Pour over 250 ml (9 fl oz/1 cup) stock or enough to just cover the meat. Cut a sheet of baking paper to fit over the meat. Cover with a lid. Bake for 1 hour 30 minutes, or until the veal is very tender.

To make the gremolata, combine all the ingredients. Carefully remove the cooked meat from the casserole dish and boil the sauce for 5–10 minutes, or until reduced a little and syrupy. Spoon off any surface fat.

To serve, put the osso buco on serving plates, top with some sauce and sprinkle with gremolata. Serve with pasta.

garam masala

makes 4 tablespoons

10 **cardamom pods**

1 **cinnamon stick**

2 tablespoons **cumin seeds**

2 teaspoons **cloves**

1 teaspoon **black peppercorns**

1 teaspoon freshly grated **nutmeg**

Remove the seeds from the cardamom pods and discard the pods. Break the cinnamon stick into small pieces. Put the cardamom seeds, cinnamon pieces, cumin seeds, whole cloves and black peppercorns in a small frying pan. Dry-fry for 1–2 minutes, or until aromatic. Set aside and cool. Put in a food processor or spice mill with the nutmeg and blend until finely ground.

Store in an airtight container for up to 1 month.

garam masala **blends**

A traditional **Indian** blend, which is probably one of the more familiar spice **mixes**, garam masala is available in supermarkets.

369

lentil soup

makes 8 cups

2 tablespoons **olive oil**

1 **onion**, finely chopped

1 **leek**, finely chopped

4 **garlic cloves**, finely chopped

1 tablespoon **garam masala**

1 stick **celery**, finely diced

1 **carrot**, finely diced

230 g (8 oz/1¼ cups) **brown lentils**

400 g (14 oz) tin **chopped tomatoes**

1 tablespoon **tomato paste (concentrated purée)**

1.75 litres (61 fl oz/7 cups) **chicken** or **vegetable stock**

2 large sprigs **thyme**

2 tablespoons chopped **parsley**, to serve

grated **parmesan cheese**, to serve

Heat the oil in a large heavy-based saucepan. Add the onion, leek and garlic. Cook and stir for 2 minutes. Add the garam masala and cook for a further 2 minutes. Stir in the celery and carrot. Cover and cook, stirring two or three times, over low heat for 10 minutes, or until the vegetables are softened.

Add the lentils and stir to coat in the vegetables. Add the tomatoes, tomato paste, stock and thyme sprigs. Bring to the boil, then lower the heat and simmer for 50 minutes, stirring occasionally, or until the lentils are tender. If evaporating too rapidly, add a little more stock or water to keep the lentils covered with liquid. Remove the thyme sprigs. Season well with salt and black pepper. Serve hot sprinkled with parsley and parmesan.

tip This soup is very thick, you can thin it with a little stock or water if desired.

lamb koftas in spicy tomato sauce

serves 4

3 tablespoons **vegetable oil**

2 large **onions**, finely chopped

3 **garlic cloves**, finely chopped

1½ tablespoons **garam masala**

½ teaspoon **chilli powder**

400 g (14 oz) tin **chopped tomatoes**

1 tablespoon **tomato paste (concentrated purée)**

500 ml (17 fl oz/2 cups) **beef stock**

270 ml (9½ fl oz) tin **coconut milk**

500 g (1 lb 2 oz) **minced (ground) lamb**

1 large handful **mint**, finely chopped, plus extra, to garnish

1 large handful **coriander (cilantro) leaves**, finely chopped, plus extra, to garnish

1 **egg**, lightly beaten

juice of 1 **lime**

steamed basmati rice, to serve

Heat the oil in a large heavy-based frying pan. Cook the onion for 5 minutes, or until lightly brown. Add the garlic, garam masala and chilli powder. Cook, stirring for 2–3 minutes, or until aromatic. Remove half of the onion mixture to a large bowl and set aside to cool.

Add the chopped tomatoes and tomato paste to the remaining onion in the frying pan, stirring. Simmer for 5 minutes, then add the stock and coconut milk. Bring to the boil, then remove from the heat, cover and set aside.

Add the minced lamb, herbs and beaten egg to the cooled onion mixture. With clean wet hands, roll the meat into 28 walnut-sized balls. Cover and refrigerate for 30 minutes to allow the flavours to develop.

Heat the sauce to simmering point. Add the kofta balls and cook over low heat for 1 hour, or until cooked through and the sauce has reduced and thickened. Gently stir the kofta balls occasionally. Stir in the lime juice. Garnish with the extra herbs and serve with basmati rice.

quatre épices

makes 2 tablespoons

1 tablespoon whole **white peppercorns**

1 teaspoon **cloves**

1 teaspoon freshly grated **nutmeg**

1/2 teaspoon **ground ginger**

Dry-fry the peppercorns and cloves in a small frying pan over medium heat for 1–2 minutes, or until aromatic. Cool. Put in a food processor with the nutmeg and ginger and blend until finely ground.

Store in an airtight container for up to 1 month.

A traditional European spice **blend**, mostly used when preparing preserved meats. The name literally means four **spices**.

rabbit and mushroom rillettes

serves 8

1 **rabbit**, skinned and cleaned
(about 350 g/12 oz)
750 g (1 lb 10 oz) **pork belly**, bones
and rind removed
500 g (1 lb 2 oz) **pork belly fat**
50 g (13/4 oz) **button mushrooms**,
finely sliced

10 g (1/4 oz) **porcini mushrooms**
2 teaspoons **quatre épices**
1 **garlic clove**, crushed
125 ml (4 fl oz/1/2 cup) **white wine**
thyme, to garnish (optional)
toast, to serve

Preheat the oven to 120°C (235°F/Gas 1/2). Wash and pat dry the rabbit with paper towel. Chop into four pieces. Cut the pork belly into large pieces and the pork belly fat into small cubes. Put all the meat, pork fat and button mushrooms into a 3 litre (104 fl oz/12 cup) capacity casserole dish.

Put the porcini mushrooms into a small bowl and cover with 125 ml (4 fl oz/1/2 cup) of hot water. Set aside for 5 minutes. Squeeze dry and cut the porcini mushrooms into smaller pieces. Retain the soaking liquid. Return the porcini mushrooms to the soaking liquid. Add the quatre épices, garlic and the wine. Mix to combine, then pour over the meats and button mushrooms. Use clean hands to thoroughly combine.

Put on a tight-fitting lid and bake for 4 hours, or until the meat is soft and falls off the bone. Season with salt and black pepper. Put all the contents of the dish into a large sieve over a bowl. Allow the fat and juices to seep through, and reserve.

When cool, remove and discard the bones from the rabbit. Use two forks to finely shred the rabbit and pork belly meats. Discard the fat from the pork belly. Put the shredded meats into eight 125 ml (4 fl oz/1/2 cup) ramekins. Strain the reserved fat and juices then pour over the meat to cover well. Seal and refrigerate for 1 day to allow the flavours to mature. To serve, turn out of the ramekins, garnish with thyme and serve with toast.

tips The rillettes will keep refrigerated for up to 2 weeks. Keep the meat well covered with the fat.

old-fashioned pork and veal pies

makes 6

400 g (14 oz) **pork**, finely diced

400 g (14 oz) **veal**, finely diced

1 small **green apple**, peeled, cored, and finely diced

50 g (13/4 oz/1/3 cup) **pistachio nuts**, roughly chopped

2 tablespoons chopped **parsley**

1 tablespoon **thyme**

3 teaspoons **quatre épices**

hot water pastry

560 g (1 lb 4 oz/41/2 cups) **plain (all-purpose) flour**

160 g (53/4 oz) **butter**, cut into cubes

2 **eggs**, lightly beaten

1 **egg yolk**, for brushing

125 ml (4 fl oz/1/2 cup) **apple juice**

11/2 teaspoons **gelatine powder**

Put the pork, veal, apple, pistachio nuts, herbs and quatre épices in a large bowl. Thoroughly mix using clean hands. Cover and refrigerate.

Grease six 250 ml (9 fl oz/1 cup) muffin holes. To make the pastry, put the flour into a large bowl. Season well with salt. Melt the butter with 170 ml (51/2 fl oz/2/3 cup) of water in a saucepan and bring to the boil. Add to the flour mixture with the eggs. Knead to form a smooth dough.

Preheat the oven to 200°C (400°F/Gas 6). Take two-thirds of the pastry (keep the remaining one-third covered) and divide into six portions. Roll each into a large circle to fit the muffin holes. Leave a little hanging over the top. Fill the pastry with the filling, packing evenly and forming a slight dome. Divide the remaining pastry into six portions. Roll each out and cut into a 12 cm (41/2 inch) circle using a pastry cutter and cut a 1.5 cm (5/8 inch) hole in the centre. Brush water around the edge of the base pastry, then place on the tops. Pinch together the overhanging edges and tops. Mix the egg yolk with 2 teaspoons of water and brush the pastry tops.

Bake on a baking tray for 40 minutes. Cover with foil. Remove from the oven and set aside for 5 minutes. Line the baking tray with baking paper then remove the pies from the tin. Bake a further 20 minutes, or until evenly browned.

Put the apple juice in a saucepan. Sprinkle over the gelatine and leave to go spongy. Add 185 ml (6 fl oz/3/4 cup) of water and heat to dissolve the gelatine. Put a small funnel over the hole in the pie and carefully pour in the liquid. Cover and refrigerate overnight.

pickling spices

makes 1/3 cup

12 **dried bird's eye chillies**

1 teaspoon **yellow mustard seeds**

1 teaspoon **fennel seeds**

1 teaspoon **dill seeds**

1 teaspoon **allspice**

1 teaspoon **cloves**

1 teaspoon **juniper berries**

4 **dried bay leaves**, crushed

1 **cinnamon stick**, broken into small pieces

Put all the spices in a small bowl and combine well.

Store in an airtight container for up to 1 month.

A mixture used for
pickling and making
preserves. Many
different **variations**
can be used according to
specific recipes.

381

onion marmalade

makes 630 g (1 lb 6 oz/2 cups)

1 kg (2 lb 4 oz) large **red onions**, cut in half and finely sliced

1 tablespoon **pickling spices**

375 ml (13 fl oz/1 1/2 cups) **malt vinegar**

460 g (1 lb/2 1/2 cups) **soft brown sugar**

2 large sprigs **thyme**

Put the onion slices in a large heavy-based saucepan. Put the pickling spices in a square of muslin (cheesecloth) and secure with string. Add the muslin bag and the malt vinegar to the saucepan. Bring to the boil then lower the heat and simmer for 45 minutes, stirring frequently, or until the onion is very soft.

Add the sugar and thyme sprigs, and season with salt and black pepper. Stir to dissolve the sugar. Bring to the boil then lower the heat and simmer for 20 minutes, or until thick and syrupy. Remove the muslin bag and thyme sprigs.

Spoon, while hot, into clean, warm sterilized jars and seal. Leave for 2 weeks to allow the flavour to develop. Store in a cool dark place and use within 6 months. Refrigerate after opening.

watermelon rind pickle

makes 5 cups

4 kg (9 lb) **watermelon**

35 g (1 1/4 oz/1/4 cup) **salt**

1 tablespoon **pickling spices**

1.25 litres (44 fl oz/5 cups) **cider vinegar**

1 kg (2 lb 4 oz) **sugar**

2 **lemons**

Remove the outer skin and pink flesh from the watermelon and discard. Cut the remaining white rind into thin strips, leaving a little bit of pink, then into 2 cm (3/4 inch) pieces. Put in a large bowl, cover with cold water and stir in the salt. Cover and stand overnight.

Drain and rinse. Put the rind in a large non-reactive saucepan, cover with cold water and bring to the boil. Cook for 20 minutes, or until the rind has softened, then drain.

Put the pickling spices in a square of muslin (cheesecloth) and secure with string. Put the muslin bag, the cider vinegar and 250 ml (9 fl oz/1 cup) of water and the sugar into the saucepan. Bring to the boil, stirring to dissolve the sugar, then boil for 5 minutes. Cut the skin and flesh from one lemon into fine slices and juice the remaining lemon.

Return the melon to the saucepan and add the lemon slices and juice. Bring back to the boil then boil for 45 minutes, or until the mixture is thick and syrupy and the rind is transparent. Discard the muslin bag.

Spoon, while hot, into clean warm sterilized jars and seal. Leave for 2 weeks to allow the flavour to develop. Store in a cool dark place and use within 6 months. Refrigerate after opening.

mixed spice

makes 2 tablespoons

1 tablespoon **ground cinnamon**

1 teaspoon **ground coriander**

1 teaspoon **ground nutmeg**

1/2 teaspoon **ground ginger**

1/4 teaspoon **ground allspice**

1/4 teaspoon **ground cloves**

Put all the spices in a small bowl and combine well.

Store in an airtight container for up to 1 month.

A combination of spices

used in **sweet** cookery,

usually in classic recipes

for **cakes**, puddings

and biscuits (cookies).

bread and butter pudding

serves 4–6

30 g (1 oz) **butter**, softened

8 slices **white bread**

2 tablespoons **caster (superfine) sugar**

2 teaspoons **mixed spice**

90 g (3¼ oz/½ cup) **pitted dried dates**, chopped

3 **eggs**

2 tablespoons **caster (superfine) sugar**, extra

1 teaspoon grated **lemon zest**

250 ml (9 fl oz/1 cup) **cream (whipping)**, plus extra to serve

250 ml (9 fl oz/1 cup) **milk**

80 g (2¾ oz/¼ cup) **apricot jam**

Lightly grease a shallow baking dish. Lightly butter the bread and cut each slice into four triangles, leaving the crusts on. Combine the caster sugar and mixed spice in a small bowl.

Arrange half the bread triangles over the dish, sprinkling with all the chopped dates and half the combined sugar and mixed spice. Arrange the remaining bread over the top and sprinkle over the remaining sugar mixture.

Preheat the oven to 180°C (350°F/Gas 4). Put a baking tin in the oven and half-fill it with hot water.

In a large bowl, whisk together the eggs, extra sugar and lemon zest. Put the cream and milk in a small saucepan and bring slowly to the boil. Immediately whisk into the egg mixture, then pour over the bread slices. Set aside for 20 minutes to allow the bread to absorb the liquid.

Cover the pudding loosely with foil. Bake in the water bath for 15 minutes. Remove the foil and bake for a further 15 minutes, or until golden brown.

Warm the jam in a microwave or in a small saucepan. Use a pastry brush to coat the top of the pudding with the jam. Return to the oven for 5 minutes. Serve with cream.

panforte

makes about 40 pieces

155 g (5^1/2 oz/1 cup) **blanched almonds**

140 g (5 oz/1 cup) **hazelnuts**

edible rice paper, to line a 26 x 17 cm (10^1/2 x 6^1/2 inch) rectangular tin

90 g (3^1/4 oz/^{3}/4 cup) **plain (all-purpose) flour**

1 tablespoon **mixed spice**

240 g (8^1/2 oz/1 cup) chopped **mixed glacé fruit**

60 g (2^1/4 oz/^{1}/3 cup) **mixed peel**, chopped (optional)

95 g (3^1/4 oz/^{1}/2 cup) chopped **dried figs**

175 g (6 oz/^{1}/2 cup) **honey**

115 g (4 oz/^{1}/2 cup) **caster (superfine) sugar**

icing (confectioners') sugar, for sprinkling

Preheat the oven to 180°C (350°F/Gas 4). Spread the almonds onto a baking tray and bake for 3–4 minutes, or until lightly golden. Roast the hazelnuts separately for 5 minutes, then rub off the skins in a clean tea towel (dish towel).

Reduce the oven temperature to 150°C (300°F/Gas 2). Line a 26 x 17 cm (10^1/2 x 6^1/2 inch) rectangular tin with edible rice paper. Sift the flour and mixed spice into a large bowl. Add the nuts, glacé and dried fruits. Coat the nuts and fruit in the flour.

Put the honey and caster sugar in a small saucepan. Stir over low heat until dissolved. Brush down the sides of the saucepan with a wet pastry brush to ensure all the sugar has dissolved. Bring to the boil then remove from the heat.

Pour the hot mixture over the flour mixture and thoroughly mix. Press into the prepared tin, using wet fingers to spread. Bake for 30 minutes, or until firm to touch. Cool, then coat liberally with sifted icing sugar. Cover with foil and leave for 2–3 days to allow the flavour to develop. Cut into small squares or triangles to serve.

tip Use two or three varieties of glacé fruits, such as pineapple, apricots and pears. Keep covered and refrigerated. This panforte will keep for 1 month.

index

Published by Murdoch Books Pty Limited

Murdoch Books Australia
Pier 8/9, 23 Hickson Road, Millers Point NSW 2000
Phone: +61 (0)2 8220 2000 Fax: +61 (0)2 8220 2558
www.murdochbooks.com.au

Murdoch Books UK Limited
Erico House, 6th Floor North, 93–99 Upper Richmond Road
Putney, London SW15 2TG
Phone: + 44 (0)20 8785 5995 Fax: + 44 (0)20 8785 5985

Chief Executive: Juliet Rogers
Publisher: Kay Scarlett

Design manager: Vivien Valk
Project manager: Paul McNally
Editor: Gordana Trifunovic
Food editor: Tracy Rutherford
Text: Paul McNally
Designer: Jacqueline Richards
Photographer: Jared Fowler
Stylist: Cherise Koch
Food preparation: Alan Wilson
Recipes by: Emma Braz, Michelle Earl, Vicky Harris, Theressa Klein, Jane Lawson,
Michelle Lucia, Kim Meredith, Louise Pickford, Alison Roberts, Tracy Rutherford,
Mandy Sinclair, Kerrie Sun, Abi Ulgiati, Mary Wills.
Production: Adele Troeger

National Library of Australia Cataloguing-in-Publication Data: Spice it. Includes index.
ISBN 1 74045 601 7. 1. Cookery (Spices). 641.6383

IMPORTANT: Those who might be at risk from the effects of salmonella poisoning (the elderly,
pregnant women, young children and those suffering from immune deficiency diseases) should
consult their doctor with any concerns about eating raw eggs.
CONVERSION GUIDE: You may find cooking times vary depending on the oven you are using.
For fan-forced ovens, as a general rule, set the oven temperature to 20°C (35°F) lower
than indicated in the recipe. We have used 20 ml (4 teaspoon) tablespoon measures. If you are
using a 15 ml (3 teaspoon) tablespoon, for most recipes the difference will not be noticeable.